Ethnic Violence
and Justice

Ethnic Violence and Justice
is based on the transcript of a workshop organized
by the Open Society Institute and the Center for
Policy Studies at Central European University
on May 9-10, 2002, in Budapest.

Workshop Chairman:
Aryeh Neier

Workshop Principal Speakers and OSI Fellows:
Fred Abrahams
Bill Berkeley
Joost Hiltermann
Dinah PoKempner
Samantha Power
David Rohde

Ethnic Violence and Justice

The Debate over Responsibility,
Accountability, Intervention,
Complicity, Tribunals,
and Truth Commissions

Open Society Institute
and the Center for Policy Studies
at Central European University

CEU PRESS

Central European University Press
Budapest — New York

Copyright © Open Society Institute, 2003

Published by Central European University Press

An imprint of the Central European University Share Company
Nádor utca 11, H-1051 Budapest, Hungary
Tel: +36 1 327 3138 or 327 3000
Fax: +36 1 327 3183
E-mail: ceupress@ceu.hu
Website: www.ceupress.com

400 West 59th Street, New York, NY 10019 USA
Tel: +1 212 547 6932
Fax: +1 212 548 4607
E-mail: mgreenwald@sorosny.org

Produced by the
Open Society Institute's Communications Office
in New York and the
Center for Policy Studies at
Central European University

ISBN 963 9241 74 1

Library of Congress
Cataloging-in-Publication Data
Library of Congress Cataloging-in-Publication Data

Ethnic violence and justice : the debate over responsibility, accountability,
intervention, complicity, tribunals, and truth commissions.
p. cm.
Edited transcript of a workshop held May 9-10, 2002, by the Open Society Institute
and the Center for Policy Studies at Central European University.
ISBN (Paperback)
1. Political violence–Congresses. 2. Ethnic relations–Political aspects–Congresses.
3. Human rights–Congresses. I. Open Society Institute. II. Center for Policy Studies. III. Title.
JC328.6.E876 2003
305.8--dc21
                    2003010862

Design by Balázs Czeizel
Layout by Judit Kovács · Createch Ltd.
Printed by Createch Ltd.

Contents

Foreword

How should the outside world have reacted when women and children were herded into churches and burned to death in Rwanda? Or when some 6,000 men were murdered in Srebrenica? How should it deal with the ongoing slaughter and enslavement in Sudan, where some two million people have died over the past two decades? Are the Khmer Rouge alone responsible for Cambodia's killing fields? Are diplomats, business people, and distant political leaders accountable when strongmen in places like Somalia, Sierra Leone, Liberia, and Congo resort to mass murder to seize and maintain power? Do the governments that provided arms and loans to Iraq bear part of the responsibility for Saddam Hussein's chemical weapons attacks on Kurdish towns?

The unparalleled killing and destruction of the last century left an indelible scar on the world's population. In many wars, the targeting of civilians to the point of near extinction was used as a strategic tactic. And this phenomenon was named genocide.

These terrible events prompted a more sophisticated understanding of human rights. The United Nations adopted the Genocide Convention on December 9, 1948, and on the following day passed the Universal Declaration of Human Rights. Yet a significant organized human rights movement did not emerge as a political force until three decades later. Activists recorded human rights abuses across the globe –an important step in making the guilty accountable. Although the human rights movement has met mixed success in convincing international powers to respond to abuses, it has succeeded in creating a crucial discourse on the role of the outside world in the face of atrocity. The debate is still evolving within human rights circles and beyond.

To explore these issues, the Open Society Institute (OSI) and Central European University (CEU) on May 9-10, 2002, held a workshop on the response of the outside world to ethnic conflict. It was the second in a series of workshops initiated by OSI Chairman George Soros to start a dialogue between OSI fellows and CEU students and faculty. The fellows were paired with CEU scholars working on similar issues. The first such workshop, which focused on U.S. civil society issues, was held in the fall of 2001. The next was to focus on international human rights issues—a broad and rather daunting topic to squeeze into a two-day conference. With input from OSI President Aryeh Neier and the six fellows attending the conference—Samantha Power, David Rohde, Joost Hiltermann, Dinah PoKempner, Bill Berkeley, and Fred Abrahams—it became clear that the conference agenda should concentrate on the overarching concepts of justice and responsibility.

The fellows had produced a critically acclaimed body of scholarly work on a range of issues connected with genocide, crimes against humanity, and the decision making that has surrounded them. The workshop gave them an opportunity to discuss their work before a distinguished group of legal professionals, scholars, and human rights advocates and investigators.

The participants exchanged views on responsibility for genocide, on personal and governmental accountability, on intervention and inaction, and on war crimes tribunals. The workshop was not intended to produce answers, as there are none. There is no one reason why ethnic violence occurs and no single formula for preventing it. War crimes tribunals and truth commissions have put the notion of responsibility on the international agenda, but they have not significantly curbed the perpetration of atrocities. The next decades may show whether the formation of an International Criminal Court, which is just getting underway, will act as a deterrent to potential perpetrators. At the beginning of the 21st century, however, the world remains wrenched by conflict with no end in sight.

This publication is the offspring of an informed discussion of the many issues surrounding the massive violations of human rights that have marred the past century and the international community's wholly inadequate responses to them. The pages that follow contain an edited version of this discussion.

Laura Silber
Senior Policy Advisor
Open Society Institute
New York

Workshop Chairman:

Aryeh Neier, president, Open Society Institute, and author of *War Crimes: Brutality, Genocide, Terror and the Struggle for Justice*, among other books.

OSI Fellowship Recipients and Workshop Speakers:

Fred Abrahams is currently writing a book on the social and political developments in Albania from 1990 to 2000. As a researcher at Human Rights Watch, he covered Albania, Macedonia, and Kosovo for five years, including the period of the Serbian ethnic-cleansing operations and the NATO air strikes. He also contributed to the Kosovo war crimes investigation for the prosecutor's office at the United Nations International Criminal Tribunal for the Former Yugoslavia in The Hague.

Bill Berkeley has been an editorial writer at the *New York Times* and for more than a decade reported on African affairs for the *Atlantic Monthly*, the *New Republic*, the *New York Times Magazine*, and the *Washington Post*. Berkeley is the author of *The Graves Are Not Yet Full: Race, Tribe and Power in the Heart of Africa*, which was chosen as a *Los Angeles Times* Best Book of 2001. He also teaches writing at Columbia University's School of International and Public Affairs.

Joost Hiltermann is the former executive director of the Arms Division of Human Rights Watch and an adjunct professor at Georgetown University. In June 2002, he joined the International Crisis Group as project director for the Middle East. He authored *Behind the Intifada: Labor and Women's Movements in the Occupied Territories* (1991) and served as the principal researcher for *Iraq's Crime of Genocide: The Anfal Campaign Against the Kurds* (1995). He is completing work on a book describing the consequences of the international silence about the use of chemical weapons during the Iran-Iraq war.

Dinah PoKempner is the general counsel at Human Rights Watch and a fellow at Columbia University's School of Law. The author of numerous articles on human rights and humanitarian law, she has conducted extensive field research in Cambodia as well as the former Yugoslavia, Hong Kong, South Korea, and Vietnam. She is currently preparing the first comprehensive handbook for non-legal professionals on the production of evidence for use in prosecuting serious human rights crimes.

Samantha Power was the founding executive director of the Carr Center for Human Rights Policy at the John F. Kennedy School of Government at Harvard University (1998-2002). A former Balkan war correspondent and a graduate of Harvard Law School, she is the co-editor, along with Graham Alison, of *Realizing Human Rights: Moving from Inspiration to Impact* (2000) and author of the critically acclaimed *"A Problem from Hell": America and the Age of Genocide* (2002), for which she won a Pulitzer Prize.

David Rohde, the New Delhi bureau chief of the *New York Times*, was awarded a Pulitzer Prize in 1996 for his reporting on the massacre of Muslims in the Bosnian town of Srebrenica. He authored *Endgame* (1998), an account of the Srebrenica killings, and covered the Israeli-Palestinian violence in 2001-2002.

Justice: Different Notions of Responsibility

Moderator: *Aryeh Neier*
Welcome: *Yehuda Elkana*, president and rector, Central European University
Panelists: *Fred Abrahams, Bill Berkeley, Joost Hiltermann,*
Dinah Pokempner, Samantha Power, David Rohde
Comments: *Judge Patricia Wald*, former chief judge of the United States
Circuit Court of Appeals for the District of Columbia and former judge on the
International Criminal Tribunal for the Former Yugoslavia (ICTY)

Aryeh Neier: I am glad the title of this discussion contains the word "responsibility." Very often, discussions about what happens after terrible abuses have been committed focus on reconciliation. Reconciliation has its value. But it does not seem to me to be the most important thing that ought to arise after terrible crimes have taken place. In my view, the most important thing is that those who aided and abetted the commission of these acts and those who were bystanders should face up to their own responsibility for them. Following the thinking of the German philosopher Karl Jaspers, I would argue that, while we think of criminal responsibility as having to be individual, at least so far as political responsibility is concerned, it also has to be collective. Jaspers was an opponent of the Nazis. Nevertheless, he said that, as a German who felt himself a member of the German community, he had to face up to his own responsibility for the Nazis' crimes. He could not simply say: "I was opposed, and therefore I don't have any responsibility for what transpired."

All of us define ourselves, to an extent, by the national communities, religious communities, professional communities, and other communities to which we belong. And therefore, it has seemed to me that, as members of these communities, we have to think about what our communities did during times in which great crimes transpired. We have to recognize that, as members of these communities, we have some responsibility.

I'd like to ask the participants to think about the horrors that they have focused on during their research. I'd like them to say whether they think that what has transpired since those horrors were committed has contributed to the assuming of responsibility for those crimes or whether responsibility has been avoided by those who contributed to the crimes or stood by while the crimes were committed.

The Misuse of History for Political Purposes

Yehuda Elkana: When I came to Central European University as rector two and a half years ago, it was clear to me that a university identified with values and social responsibility must become a research university. Values and social responsibility must be rooted in proper research. And this is what we are trying to do at Central European University.

I find it curious that the situation in Palestine and Israel is not one of the conference topics. I would like to raise it, and to approach it from a non-legalistic point of view. I want to draw from my own life experience. I am an Auschwitz graduate and have been an Israeli for 50 years. But what I've seen in my life, and what I deeply believe, is that historical hatreds and events are totally irrelevant—and should be irrelevant—to politics.

What counts for me is that, at those times when there has been no Jenin and when there have been no terrorist attacks, more or less 70 percent of the people on both sides have been ready, in principle, to live in peace, side-by-side. In other words, the Israeli-Palestinian problem is a political problem.

But it might also be a legal problem. How is it possible to prevent political powers from misusing historical events systematically in order to incite hatred? For me, this is a very fundamental issue. Using history for present political purposes is one of the most awful abuses of history and mythology. So many times I have seen that when the political situation changes, these so-called deep hatreds suddenly disappear. When the political situation changes, everything is possible.

None of us predicted the last big reversal of this kind—the fall of the Berlin Wall. So, in the long run, these so-called hatreds are not so deeply ingrained that we must consider them as an ongoing catastrophe among people and conclude that nothing can be done about them. I am curious to know where the limit is to what can be done. What can or cannot be legally investigated?

Whether there was a massacre in Jenin, we don't know. I personally happen to believe that there was not. But this is neither here nor there, and not because I favor Ariel Sharon. He is a war criminal in my eyes. I wish I could see him stand before some war crimes tribunal sooner or later because of his whole history. This, however, does not mean that Yasser Arafat is my hero of integrity.

The United Nations investigation commission might have been able to answer the question of what happened in Jenin, if it had been allowed to work. But it was self-evident to me that its mandate was to study the basic facts of what happened in Jenin, to answer the question, "How many people were killed?" But it did not have the mandate to address something I believe to be beyond doubt: that the Israeli government, under Sharon, has systematically tried to destroy the civil infrastructure of the Palestinian Authority. In the long run, this is not less important. But, somehow, it is not considered, as far as I can see, when human rights and justice are brought up for discussion. And possibly it should be. It is a political and historical question. But it must, it should, make us pause.

I see you are dealing with tribunals and comparing events that have happened in various countries. I would ask how are we to deal with the fact that Germany became a successful democracy? To a great extent this had to do with the fact that Chancellor Konrad Adenauer refused to carry out in-depth de-Nazification of his country after the war. How do we deal with this fact? Is it something that can be dealt with in this kind of intellectual discourse combining legal, historical, and political thinking?

Aryeh Neier: Yehuda, when you referred to the role of history, I was reminded of Eric Hobsbawm, the historian, who said that, when he was a young man, he thought that his profession at least had the advantage of not being dangerous, like the practice of physics, for example, but that he had learned better over time.

Srebrenica: Resignations and Responsibility among the Dutch

David Rohde: As a journalist, I have a broad but superficial knowledge of these events. I do not think I have had enough time to analyze them. I will quickly run through different places I've reported from and what responsibility, if any, has been assumed in the wake of war crimes there. I actually will address Israel, and specifi-cally Jenin. Yehuda's general impression was correct. There was no massacre. But many other questionable activities went on there.

The clearest example, in terms of the question of responsibility, was Srebrenica. I still think there are problems. But there has actually been a strong sense of re-sponsibility among the Dutch peacekeepers who were there. The Dutch have issued a very large report. The Dutch government ended up resigning because one of its members felt someone had to take responsibility for what occurred in Srebrenica. In a sense it is absurd. It has taken so long, and there really has not been much fallout from it. But the Dutch have at least made an effort.

Srebrenica has really traumatized Holland as a society. There were individual Dutch commanders who made enormous mistakes in Srebrenica, and they have not been punished severely for what they did. But I'm generally impressed with Dutch society and the extent of the investigating that Dutch journalists have done. In terms of Bosnia itself, the International Criminal Tribunal for the Former Yugoslavia has made tremendous progress. But the main perpetrator of the Srebrenica massacre,

3

General Ratko Mladic, remains at large. Although I have not been to Bosnia now in several years, I sense that there is only a small sense of responsibility, particularly among Bosnian Serbs. There is still doubt among them about whether there even were massacres carried out in Srebrenica. Many people still reject the idea and the number of victims involved, which was about 7,000.

One topic that should be discussed is the success or failure of the tribunal. Is the tribunal serving the interests of the United States and the West and human rights groups? Is it actually having an impact on the ground in terms of people facing up to their responsibility? I've done work in Indonesia and Nigeria, looking at religious conflict in these countries. It is sad that so little attention is paid to these conflicts. There are very few efforts by local courts to prosecute any of the higher-level people who instigated the clashes that I saw. Usually there is an active effort from the top to incite people to attack each other. The attacks are not spontaneous, something that comes from a popular sense. They are usually much more planned, and it takes a while to condition people to actually participate.

My last point will be to address the question of responsibility in terms of Israel and the continuing cycle of violence there. Of all the conflicts I've covered, the violence in Israel is the saddest and darkest. There is tremendous hatred on both sides now. But I was most disappointed by the cynicism of the leadership on both sides, the degree to which they are locked in a death struggle, a struggle to vanquish their opponent, and the way facts are manipulated by both sides. There is far less middle ground there than I've ever seen in any conflict.

I would like to turn to the conduct of the Israeli forces and the recent incursions in Jenin. I think it is outrageous that there is no United Nations investigating team going there. Again, I do not think a massacre occurred in Jenin. But if it had been a different situation with a different government, I think there would be a much greater outcry about the blocking of the UN team.

In most of these conflicts, prosecutions do help develop a sense of responsibility, because they individualize the actors, making individuals, not groups, responsible. I know this is a theory. But I see it on the ground. It does help in terms of long-term reconciliation.

Iraq's Slaughter of Kurds: Issues of Complicity and Impunity

Joost Hiltermann: The issue of responsibility in Iraq, where we think up to 100,000 Kurds were systematically slaughtered in a five-month period in 1988, remains unresolved for two main reasons. First, the regime that committed this mass crime remains in power. So holding it accountable has been very difficult. Second, we understand from eyewitness accounts that these people were killed. But we don't actually have the physical evidence, because we have had no access to the areas where the victims have supposedly been buried. We don't actually know that they are all dead. It is extremely doubtful, but for all we know, some might still be alive, living in underground dungeons. The supposition is that they are all dead, because they have not come back to their homes.

Now, if you talk about responsibility, the question is not only who is responsible, but also who is going to hold the responsible party to account. In the case of Iraq, you have the issues of complicity and impunity.

Iraq was the perpetrator, but it received massive international support at the time for its war against Iran. This support translated into complete silence on the part of the international community when Iraq started suppressing its own dissident communities and committed other crimes in the process of prosecuting the Iran-Iraq war. At the end of that war, aid to Iraq was increased further until Iraq made the strategic error of entering Kuwait. This triggered a complete flip-flop in international policy toward Iraq, turning it from friend to foe.

Even in the 1990s, when Iraq clearly had been at the receiving end of the international community's aid, the United States in particular had huge amounts of evidence about Iraqi war crimes, provided by organizations like Human Rights Watch. The United States has failed to do anything with the evidence. I know because I have been working at Human Rights Watch and dealing with the U.S. government regarding this evidence. Some people in the State Department are very interested in taking up this issue, but they simply have not had the political support within the government to do anything of significance.

All the evidence is there to bring Iraq's leadership to trial, either at the International Court of Justice with a genocide case or through an ad hoc international tribunal. This evidence can also be used to try individual members of the regime through universal jurisdiction in particular countries like Belgium, where the issue is being considered at the moment. But nothing concrete has happened to date. Until this regime is actually held to account for its crimes, rather than its population punished for the regime's crimes, we will not see any true justice in Iraq. I'm a bit concerned. The United States has made it clear that it is going to attack Iraq and that the human rights argument will be mobilized in order to justify this war. But the real reason for the war has nothing to do with human rights or the welfare of the Iraqi people. This will undermine the prospect of actually bringing about a democratic change in Iraq.

Witnesses to War Crimes:
What Is the Responsibility of Bystanders?

Dinah PoKempner: Aryeh and I once actually managed to speak to a Khmer Rouge representative. He assured us that the Khmer Rouge respected human rights in every aspect except freedom of speech, which, at the time, couldn't be fully implemented. Since then, I have had occasion to talk to many Khmer Rouge and other Cambodians. One is struck, twenty-some years after the end of that horrible slaughter, by how complete the evasion of responsibility has been on the part of everyone who lived through it.

The only Khmer Rouge I have ever heard of taking responsibility for the horrific acts of those times is a man named Duch who was the warden of the main torture center in Phnom Penh. He seems to have unburdened himself, very unwisely, to a reporter, partly because he became a born-again Christian. To my knowledge, he is one of only two Khmer Rouge in jail and awaiting a potential trial. Duch is in a state of indefinite detention at this point.

I've come across some astonishing stories involving low-ranking Khmer Rouge village leaders, who, though not especially indecent people, were directly involved in crimes. When confronted by people they ruled over, these Khmer Rouge have said: "I'm sorry, I wasn't the leader." There is a complete, strange, psychological divesting of responsibility, which is mirrored in Cambodia by an almost complete suppression of any discussion of the period.

In a different session I will speak about how the idea of a tribunal for the Khmer Rouge came about and failed. We're in an age of tribunals, and interest in prosecution is high. The ad hoc tribunals, the creation of the International Criminal Court, and the Pinochet precedent have given activists a tremendous interest in prosecution as a way of fixing individual responsibility. And it has made me, in my current work, think about how easy it seems to be to make the case from the outside. How important are the evidence and the witnessing done by the journalists, the human rights activists, the humanitarian workers, the International Committee of the Red Cross (ICRC), and others? What role do these people have in creating stories of responsibility, of individual responsibility, that we hope to play out in some court?

Unfortunately, I have concluded that it's quite difficult to put together these cases from the outside, without an official body to investigate and to compel evidence. Most activists, when they think about trying to change a culture of impunity and bring responsibility to center-stage, want to go after big fish and not little fish. They want to get to the commander and avoid trivializing the tragedy by going after the mid- or low-level people. Getting the big fish is, of course, most difficult. You are often operating in areas where you have to prove command responsibility, not direct participation in the horrors. And command responsibility is a curious doctrine. It requires you to show that someone is liable because of things they didn't do, things they should have known, things they should have inquired about further, or things they actually knew but did not act to prevent, suppress, or punish.

Command responsibility stands in contrast to the theory of universal jurisdiction, which states that some crimes are so harmful to humanity that every nation has a duty to prevent, suppress, and punish. Command responsibility revolves around the unique control of a particular commander, whereas universal jurisdiction says everybody is responsible. Of course, where everyone is responsible, nobody feels very much pressure to act.

But, these thoughts about responsibility have also made me think about responsibilities that are not legal yet are relevant to the legal process. These are the responsibilities of important bystanders, people who are in some way situated to be professional witnesses, the journalists on the scene, the activists, the humanitarian workers, the ICRC—the crowd that is usually present during these conflicts. Do they have, if not a legal responsibility, perhaps a moral responsibility not to just witness but to act, either at the time or later? Do they have a responsibility to prevent, and punish, and suppress, for example, by publicizing the facts of an atrocity so that the commanders know that their duty is actively to prevent, suppress, and punish?

These are my preliminary thoughts. Some of the panelists will say that perhaps I am putting too much of a burden on bystanders. But this is a different way of thinking about the role of witnesses in these situations.

America and Genocide: See Nothing, Do Nothing

Samantha Power: I had the benefit of beginning research for a book on American responses to genocide after David and Joost and Dinah and Aryeh and Fred and Bill had made such extraordinary contributions to documenting the crimes themselves. So I had, in a way, the easy part: to build on their records, to understand how American officials, believing themselves to be decent individuals who would respond in a responsible way when confronted by genocide, actually shut down when genocide or mass atrocities against civilians arose. I also tried to discover and understand the stories they told themselves to overcome the kind of moral dissonance that you would think they would experience.

There are two ways that I think about responsibility from the standpoint of bystanders—here I speak not of bystanders on the scene, but rather of people who are nowhere near the scene. These people might feel two types of responsibility. The first is the sense of responsibility to prevent or stop genocide. The second is the sense of responsibility for having allowed genocide after the fact. In neither of these aspects does one encounter—and I'll just speak here on the basis of the country I know, the United States—a sense of responsibility sufficient to mobilize a political willingness to stop genocide.

I'll take the first kind of responsibility first: the idea that we are responsible for stopping genocide as it is happening. By "we" I mean we as outsiders, say an American government, say presidents who ritually commit to remembering the Holocaust and to "never again" allowing genocide, say Americans who visit the Holocaust monument on the Mall in Washington. There is a kind of societal consensus that genocide stands atop the hierarchy of the horrible, that it warrants a very, very special response, that a duty attaches to it. Not just a right to intervene, but a duty. This is an abstract conception, and it does not mobilize people when atrocity confronts them. Let's take Rwanda in the context of the abstract notion that genocide is a bad thing, that we have a duty to stop it and not to stand idly by. In this instance, there were many, more forceful political and geopolitical reasons for not getting involved.

So, while there is a sense of a universal duty in the face of a crime of such a magnitude, it lacks political gravitas. There is evidence that people are much more apt to stop on a country lane to help a stranded motorist than they would be if the stranded motorist were on a highway. This is because people on a country lane feel like they're the only person who can help, even if it really presents a much greater danger to them personally. On a country lane, they are alone; on a highway, they would be within sight of other motorists. It is much the same thing with genocide. When it occurs, it occurs in front of everyone, and genocide does not get people out onto the streets. The reasons for not getting involved are far more persuasive.

I would like now to pick up on Joost's point about responsibility for holding people responsible. We witnessed the birth, or at least the growth, of this concept in the 1990s, with regards to the perpetrators of atrocities. This second form of responsibility—the sense of responsibility for having allowed genocide after the fact—doesn't really exist in the United States. There are no congressional investigations for sins of omission in the way that you would have for sins of commission. Surprisingly, there is little journalistic documentation or naming of those persons who made decisions not to act. The traces disappear. And the paper trail is harder to establish. As a result, there is no risk to the reputations of those who stand by, whereas there are considerable risks to taking a stand and for trying to generate interest in responding to genocide.

David mentioned the 7,600-page Dutch report on Srebrenica. This report is actually quite consistent with the European tendency to be a little bit present. Take the

French role in Srebrenica, the Belgian role in Rwanda, the French role in Rwanda, the Dutch role in Srebrenica, and, in a non-European example, the Canadian sins of commission in Somalia. In each instance, there was an international presence. The reports written about the events tend to pull back, to look at either what was done illegally or what crimes were committed or what wasn't done. Most of these reports were whitewashes. But I've come to believe that whitewashes are better than nothing. At least they have the potential to create, in the minds of policymakers and others, a fear that they might be named in a subsequent report. The United States was so absent from the scenes of these crimes that there are no reports. You weren't present; you didn't "do anything." There is no form of institutional or formal accountability. This is unfortunate.

Collective Responsibility, Individual Criminal Accountability

Fred Abrahams: I want to take a slightly different approach to this topic for purely selfish reasons. I consider myself more of a fact-finder and researcher than an analyst. And I am definitely not a lawyer. My point is that before we speak about responsibility, we must establish the facts on the ground. And they are not always so clear.

The example of Jenin is the most obvious one. There are claims, counter-claims, and maneuverings, and it is not easy to establish the truth, to discover who did what to whom. Conflicts are much more complicated today. You have shifting front lines, a multitude of combatants and different armed groups, and an increasing dynamic of local, national, regional, and international politics, like a four-tiered chess game. And all of these require our consideration. At the same time, we're overrun with images of war crimes. Our human rights community has a difficult job. It is a challenge to present the material in an objective and credible way that will have an impact on policymakers and the public.

I am also interested in discovering and utilizing new methods and technologies to document and present war crimes. These include the use of video and photography, high-speed communications from the field, and science. I would highlight what I think is a very important and interesting development in the Milosevic trial: the testimony of Patrick Ball, a scientist who used statistics to reveal the patterns of expulsion, suggesting that the ethnic cleansing of Kosovo was a coordinated campaign, rather than a random exodus. Such methodologies can be used to document the information in a compelling and objective way.

I say this to get at the question of collective responsibility. The road to collective responsibility goes through criminal accountability. And how crucial it is to identify the individual perpetrators responsible for serious crimes en route to a more thoughtful and thorough discussion of collective responsibility. More than any other conflicts, perhaps, the wars in the Balkans have produced an immense amount of work on criminal accountability because of the tribunal, human rights groups and journalists, and the intense attention that the conflicts in Croatia, Bosnia, and Kosovo received. I cannot say how much of a sense of collective responsibility exists in the Balkans or how aware local communities are about the crimes that were committed during these wars. But I would not be completely pessimistic. I do believe a lot has been done and that Serbia is changing, moving in the right direction. But I certainly believe more could be done. There are many areas, for example, where the tribunal has failed to have the desired impact on the ground and in promoting the kind of thinking that may lead toward reconciliation.

I disagree with my fellow panelists about the Dutch report. I expected more from the report. I was disappointed. I would agree that a whitewash is better than nothing. But quite frankly, I thought the report was way too little, way too late. The resignation of the government just before the Dutch elections struck me as disingenuous. We expect a little more from the Dutch. We should praise them for undertaking the investigation. But I think the report could have been much more thorough and self-critical.

Rwanda Massacres: State-orchestrated Genocide, Not Ancient Hatreds

Bill Berkeley: Let me begin by making a couple of general comments about Africa. My book is about a half-dozen conflicts in Africa: Liberia, Congo-Zaire, South Africa in the late 80s-early 90s, Sudan, Uganda, and Rwanda. These are conflicts where tens of thousands of civilians have been murdered. Horrendous wars.

Samantha has spoken a little bit about Rwanda. It is now widely understood around the world, certainly in the West, that the Rwanda massacres were not the result of ancient hatreds. They were not exotic in nature. They were the result of calculated tyranny—a state-orchestrated genocide. What is less well understood, outside of Africa, is that all of these conflicts are political conflicts, orchestrated from above, not just in an immediate context of lawlessness, but within a long history of lawless tyranny. So the issue of responsibility is a fundamental one throughout Africa. And indeed Africans themselves across a broad spectrum—during the twenty-plus years that I've been traveling to their continent—well understand this.

In fact, the African continent is the scene of a number of experiments in accountability that have not been widely covered. They underline the complexity of the problem of accountability. Perhaps the best-known example is the International Criminal Tribunal for Rwanda in Arusha. It has had very mixed results, but it is an attempt by the international community, in league with Rwandans and other Africans, to hold the top leadership of the genocide accountable. My own view of the Rwanda tribunal is that it has had a mixed record of success so far But, if nothing else, it represents a recognition by the international community that the roots of these conflicts do not lie in some cultural predisposition to violence in Africa. Rather they belong to a context of lawlessness and criminality that has overtaken much of the continent.

There have been other examples as well, across Africa, and elsewhere. In the case of Rwanda, a Belgian criminal trial convicted four nuns last year of complicity in the genocide. In Rwanda itself, there have been trials of extremely limited credibility, attempts to hold accountable more than 100,000 civilians accused of participating in the massacres in 1994. These highlight the near impossibility of an extremely poor country with limited wherewithal emerging from a war and holding accountable its own citizens. South Africa has had a truth commission, which was widely covered and which attempted to document, for the historical record at least, crimes committed during the apartheid era and to name those persons responsible for them. Back in 1996, in a criminal trial, Nelson Mandela's government attempted and failed to hold accountable top military and intelligence officials and their black collaborators for the political violence that claimed the lives of about 20,000 black South African civilians in the late 1980s and early 1990s.

There is the case of the so-called African Pinochet, Hissene Habre, the former Chadian dictator, who was indicted in Senegal; the Senegalese government managed to have that case disposed of without a trial. Another example is the new tribunal being set up in Sierra Leone to try Foday Sankoh, the rebel leader arrested a couple of years ago, and some of his allies for horrific crimes committed in the 1990s. This is a tribunal with both an international and a local component. One of the hopes for this tribunal is that, it may one day provide a forum for the indictment of Charles Taylor, the Liberian head of state, who has been the principal cause of continuing warfare that has claimed the lives of some 150,000 civilians over the last decade in West Africa. [Editor's note: The tribunal indicted Taylor in June 2003.]

Charles Taylor is a case study in the importance of accountability and responsibility in an African conflict.

Freed American slaves founded Liberia in the 19th century. The descendants of these freed slaves dominated the country for the better part of a century. In 1980, a 28-year-old soldier named Samuel Doe took over the country. In the mid-1980s, he brazenly stole an election. Just a few weeks later, a failed coup attempt brought about widespread massacres in which Doe's militia murdered hundreds of his opponents.

There was an ethnic component to these massacres. Doe was from a small minority known as the Krahn. Most of his opponents, who were suspected of being involved in the coup, were from another minority called the Gio. Krahn soldiers murdered hundreds of Gio. There was never an investigation. No one was held accountable. There were no trials, no truth commissions. Samuel Doe never acknowledged that anything had gone wrong. And five years later, a new individual whom no one had ever heard of, Charles Taylor, emerged on the scene. He was neither Krahn nor Gio, but a descendant of the freed American slaves who had founded the country. Taylor seized upon the grievances of the Gio, anticipating that the Gio, in the absence of any accountability or responsibility for the massacres five years earlier, were bent on revenge. He mobilized a handful of these Gio fighters, and with his battle cry "Kill the Krahn," staged a series of attacks.

Doe responded with counterattacks that killed large numbers of Gio civilians. Then Charles Taylor mobilized the orphans of those casualties, many of them children as young as nine or ten, and armed them and sent them into battle, again with the battle cry "Kill the Krahn." In a matter of a year, Taylor's forces murdered tens of thousands of Krahn.

I met Taylor in 1992. He had just given a speech in a ramshackle assembly hall in a town known as Buchanan, on the West African coast. There were posters along the walls of the assembly hall saying, "Let's forget the past!" Having exploited the past for his own purposes, he was now proclaiming, "Let's forget the past!" Taylor seized power in 1997, and he is now West Africa's dominant warlord. He is also West Africa's principal gunrunner, a classic example of someone, essentially a war criminal and a gangster, who has thrived in an environment of lawlessness.

In Liberia, as elsewhere in Africa, Americans played a very important role over many decades in financing and arming and legitimizing fundamentally illegitimate governments. In the 1980s, during the Reagan administration, Chester Crocker, the assistant secretary of state for Africa, played an important role in legitimizing Samuel Doe's government at a time when the United States was paying a third of Liberia's budget. Many Liberians to this day would gladly see Chester Crocker tried as a war criminal. But in Washington, Crocker is the chairman of the United States Institute for Peace, a distinguished elder statesman whose role in Liberia is long forgotten, if it was ever even noticed in America at the time.

I interviewed Chester Crocker in his office at Georgetown University in 1997. I asked him about his role in propping up and legitimizing Samuel Doe's military dictatorship at a time when that dictatorship was sowing the seeds of terrible bloodshed. This is what he said: "I would never in a million years tell you I was seeking what was in the best interest of Liberia. I was protecting the interest of Washington." So, from the standpoint of the United States' responsibility for its own role in Africa:

completely nil. I say that not to point the finger just at Chester Crocker but really at all Americans, because most Americans pay virtually no attention to the role that our country has played in Africa.

A Sense of Victimization, An Evasion of Responsibility

Aryeh Neier: While listening to the members of the panel, I found it striking that, except for the Dutch, who were bystanders rather than perpetrators in Srebrenica, we really haven't had any examples of someone feeling a strong sense of responsibility for great crimes, either because of who the perpetrators were or because of their role as bystanders.

One of the questions this raises in my mind is whether an important factor in the failure of perpetrators to face up to their responsibility is that many of the perpetrators feel themselves to be victims. Are they not ready to acknowledge the crimes that they or their forces committed, because their sense of their own victimization stands in the way of recognition of responsibility?

In the wars in ex-Yugoslavia, it has seemed to me that everybody feels that they have been victimized. Fred says there is some change taking place in Serbia. I think he is right. But it still seems to me that, by and large, Serbs continue to think of themselves as victims. With respect to Rwanda, my impression is that Hutus think of themselves as victims and therefore do not face up to their responsibility. I would like members of the panel to react to whether this sense of victimization is a factor and how much it seems to many people, whether in the Israeli-Palestinian conflict or elsewhere, to legitimize them or their forces in committing great crimes.

David Rohde: The sense of victimization plays a tremendous role on each side of the Israeli-Palestinian conflict. In all the conflicts I've reported on, I've never seen such strenuous efforts by each side to show that it, obviously, is the victim. You can't even get them to agree on a basic fact. You can present both sides with the videotape of an event, and one side will say it is fake, and the other side won't believe it. I think the sense of victimization is a huge issue in all the conflicts we've talked about.

One important point is that this culture of victimhood is now very widespread in the United States after the events of September 11. It is an enormously dangerous trend.

I will continue to give the Dutch credit, because it is important to find positive examples and to try to figure out what leads a society to take responsibility for what it has done. I don't know if we have to go all the way back to World War II to look at the German example, or to what has motivated the Dutch. Holland is a wealthy society. The Dutch joke that they are all Calvinists and that they will always punish themselves for what they have done. Obviously more could be done, but at least something has started there. In other cultures, it's just victimhood. And this is true among Americans.

Samantha Power: I think the Dutch took responsibility because the journalists and the public wouldn't go away. Organic responsibility-taking, the kind we're all wishing for, is so rare in history. It is not a problem of the 1990s. How many guilty pleas were there at Nuremberg? Around the same number as there have been at the tribunals for the former Yugoslavia and Rwanda. You can count all the guilty pleas on one hand.

We now remember the de-Nazification in Germany as being far more instantaneous than it really was. It was not the perpetrators themselves, or the collective enablers of the perpetrators, or the supporters of the perpetrators, but the German kids, the teenagers, who were rebelling and bringing out grievances against their parents in the 1960s that would prove socially constructive over time. You often see this generational lag.

We're seeing a little progress in the former Yugoslavia. The tribunal is becoming an instrument of local politics, and that is where it will do the most good. The Croatian opposition is using the tribunal to play politics locally, saying to their opponents, "Oh, you know, you're a war criminal." I think responsibility is being taken over time, but very much under duress. Let's think of our own lives: Often it takes pressure or a crisis to prompt introspection.

Getting people who have never killed before to commit crimes of this magnitude requires mobilization. And instilling a sense of victimization is a more potent mobilizing force than hate or a hunger for land or power. Everybody tells themselves a moral story. This makes it so hard, after the fact, to peel back the layers, not so much of the fact pattern, but of the very potent narrative that accompanies that fact pattern.

Politics and Responsibility: Public Pressure to Do Something

Joost Hiltermann: As the only Dutch member of the panel, I think I should say something about my personal guilt. I was going to speak on Iraq. But I will say one word about the Dutch.

There was a sense of organic responsibility. There was a lot of pressure on the government to do something. And I think the pressure arose from genuine emotions.

So the government had to act, and maybe even a couple members of the government felt personally that something ought to be done. I think the Dutch are just that way. I'm Catholic, or born Catholic anyway. But every Catholic in Holland is Calvinist really, because that is the dominant ethic. So there is this very strong ideologically bred sense of taking responsibility.

But taking responsibility doesn't translate into politics. And in terms of taking real responsibility, I think Fred was absolutely right when he said that the government's resignation was disingenuous. The government had to act. It was awfully convenient that elections were coming up and that they could resign without any real cost. In fact, by resigning just before the elections, they looked awfully good. Of course, the trauma of Srebrenica has now been overtaken by the trauma of the assassination of Pim Fortuyn, a populist, and very popular, political leader.

In Iraq, the issue is even less a communal conflict than some of the other conflicts we've been talking about here. When the Iraqi forces invaded Iran in 1980 and stayed there for two years, the conflict was very much seen as existential by the Iranian regime of the Ayatollah Khomeini. The Iranians expelled the Iraqi invaders. They did not, however, sue for peace. They chose to prosecute the war on Iraqi territory. They invaded Iraqi territory, or tried to anyway for six years before failing in the end. But from the moment of the Iranian invasion, the war became existential for Iraq. If the Iranians had succeeded in conquering the city of Basra in the south, which was their primary war aim, then the regime in Iraq might well have fallen and the entire country might have come under the domination of Iran and all that comes with it.

And so the war was very much seen as an existential war by Iraq. The Kurds, who have longstanding claims to greater autonomy and liberty in the north, took advantage of the vacuum created by the Iran-Iraq war. When Iraqi troops withdrew from the north because they were needed on the front in the south, the Kurds launched a rural insurgency. The Iraqi regime characterized this insurgency as part of the Iranian war effort, which made it part of Iraq's existential problem. The way to deal with the Kurds was not, as the Iraqi regime had done in the past, to launch a tepid counter-insurgency. Rather it was to find a final solution, the complete eradication of the rural insurgency and the rural population. This was the Anfal campaign of 1988.

Bill Berkeley: I want to make a couple of comments about the sense of victimization.

I agree with what Samantha said. Hate is nowhere near as potent a mobilizing force as a sense of victimization. But I would argue that, in the countries I have covered, the most potent of all mobilizing forces is fear. It is, in part, related to victimization, a sense that if you don't kill, you're going to be killed, and a history of victimization is cited as a rational basis for that fear. In a context of escalating violence, ordinary people who have never killed before can be convinced that it is in their rational self-interest to do so.

In the case of Rwanda, there was a history of Tutsi domination. The Tutsis were the victims of genocide in Rwanda in 1994. But historically, the Tutsis were the bad guys. They were the dominant group. And the Hutu leaders responsible for the genocide cited that history in their virulent radio propaganda, which played such an important role. The basic argument of the propagandists was that the Tutsis, and in particular a Tutsi-led rebel insurgency, were bent on retaking power and re-imposing feudalism, taking back all the land and killing all the Hutus. It is also important to remember that Rwanda is a tiny country right next to Burundi, where, during the previous two decades, Tutsis murdered large numbers of Hutus. As recently as a year before the genocide in Rwanda, Burundian Tutsis had murdered tens of thousands of Burundian Hutus. So it was possible to point the finger at widespread massacres just across the border in Burundi and say that if you don't kill Tutsis in Rwanda, the Tutsis are going to kill you.

When talking about the sense of victimization, it is important to distinguish between the political leadership, which exploits the sense of victimization for its own political purposes, and the average civilian. I think many of these leaders deliberately exploit a history of victimization for their own calculated self-interest.

Aryeh Neier: To return to the question of responsibility: The Dutch are, indeed, Calvinist; but some non-Calvinist countries and institutions have launched investigations of their role in Rwanda. There was a Belgian investigation of Belgium's role in what took place in Rwanda. There was a French investigation. The United Nations investigated its role. But there has been nothing in the United States on the U.S. role with respect to Rwanda. In fact, there has been no serious call or serious momentum for a U.S. investigation. Why is it that, at least in other places, there has been a willingness, even if the final result is at least partly a whitewash, to look at one's own record and there has not been a willingness in the United States?

Samantha Power: One way to address it is the way I did before, which is simply to say: "We weren't there."

Aryeh Neier: But we were in the UN Security Council.

Samantha Power: But none of the Security Council member states that conducted these investigations did so because they were mere members of a Security Council that sent peacekeepers into harm's way.

In the case of Rwanda, the French conducted their investigations because they had backed the regime. The Belgians conducted their investigation because Belgian peacekeepers were there and, in part, because some of them were murdered and there were cries for an explanation of how Belgian peacekeepers could have found themselves so unprepared for such hair-raising circumstances.

The UN's Srebrenica report initially named names, actually describing which official in the Department of Peacekeeping Operations made which decision at which time. At the last minute, these names were taken out. So where it might have said "Kofi Annan" as the head of the Department of Peacekeeping Operations, it just said DPKO. This led, I think, to an ironic result. When the report came out, Kofi Annan, who had gone on to become Secretary-General, was widely praised for having the courage to commission this report. But if it had actually been published as originally written, with his name in every other sentence, I think it would have generated quite a different reaction.

In the case of the United States, the excuse "We weren't there" only demands an answer to the question "Why aren't we ever there?" Part of the answer can be found in the absence of a political constituency, which ensures that there is no cost to not going or not playing or not taking any steps along the continuum of intervention. The absence of a political constituency is also evident at the time of the investigation, or during the period when the investigation should be undertaken. In the case of Rwanda, Representative Cynthia McKinney and a few other members of the Congressional Black Caucus called for investigations. But they got no support. The Clinton administration ignored their calls. Literally, McKinney would call and say, "Come, we want to summon you to speak on how you let the genocide happen." And the Clinton administration just wouldn't show up. The calls for an investigation were not picked up in the press in any meaningful way.

So there was no downside to doing nothing about the genocide, and no downside to doing nothing about investigating why we had done nothing about the genocide. We need to build these constituencies and create a political interest in looking back.

Fred Abrahams: I'd like to amplify this point. I think it largely comes down to a question of political pressure. As Joost said, in Holland there was very intense pressure on the government to address the Srebrenica issue. And such intense pressure doesn't exist in the United States. Most Americans have very little awareness of the impact United States foreign policy has on countries outside of our immediate orbit. So I guess I'm taking a cynical approach when I say that governments and international organizations will respond when they're forced to respond.

Germany and Japan:
Contrasts in Collective Political Responsibility

Aryeh Neier: I would differentiate revenge and collective political responsibility. I think an example of collective political responsibility is what has taken place in Germany over the last four decades or so. There is a widespread belief in Germany that Germans as Germans have to face up to their country's past. Even people who were not born at the time of the Holocaust feel that, as Germans, this is something that they cannot escape. I think this has had an immensely positive impact in Germany and is very much central to Germany's development as a democratic society. There are not many other places with comparable efforts. In Japan, for example, there is not a comparable sense of responsibility for the crimes that Japanese committed during World War II on an enormous scale. Probably ten million civilians were killed in Japanese war crimes in Asia, mostly in China, but also in other countries such as the Philippines and Korea.

I think the lack of a sense of collective responsibility in Japan to some degree stunted the country's democratic development. In the Japanese case, I do think that the failure to develop a sense of collective political responsibility has a great deal to do with the sense of victimization. The Japanese are, of course, aware of the firebombing of Tokyo, during which perhaps 100,000 people were killed in a single day. They are aware, of course, that the only use of nuclear weapons was against Hiroshima and Nagasaki. And if you ask Japanese people to talk about the defining event of World War II, they will refer to the dropping of the atomic bombs, affirming their portrayal of themselves as victims. I think this has prevented them from developing a sense of responsibility for the crimes committed by Japan during the war. No one, obviously, can deny that the Japanese who were burned to death in the firebombing of Tokyo and the civilians incinerated in Hiroshima and Nagasaki were victims. But these events do not cancel out what the Japanese did in China, in the rape of Nanking, or the bombing of Chungking, or other horrendous crimes.

I don't think the lack of a sense of political responsibility in Japan, or the development of a sense of political responsibility in Germany, really has anything to do with revenge. I think those are entirely different phenomena. I'm not sure I am able to explain why political responsibility developed in one country and did not develop in another. Ian Buruma has written a very good book on this question, comparing Germany and Japan. One factor in the difference is what took place in the trials after World War II. The Nuremberg trials were more significant in developing a sense of political responsibility in Germany than the Tokyo trials were in Japan.

I'll cite one example. In Tokyo, under orders from General Douglas MacArthur, there was a deliberate effort made to spare Emperor Hirohito from seeming to be responsible for what took place. MacArthur felt that Emperor Hirohito was necessary for the governance of post-war Japan and that Japan was needed as a bulwark against the advance of communism in China. Every effort was made to steer the testimony away from Hirohito. When Prime Minister Tojo said that he and the others would not have dared to act without the Emperor, he was brought back to the stand a few days later to contradict his initial testimony.

In Germany, no such political efforts were made with respect to the Nuremberg trial. After Nuremberg, there was no really meaningful de-Nazification process, as Yehuda Elkana mentioned with respect to Adenauer. But there were about 5,000 trials before German courts. I think these trials helped develop a sense of political responsibility in Germany. After the Tokyo tribunal, on the other hand, there was not a single trial of Japanese war criminals before a Japanese court. There were no national trials of war criminals. I think this is one of the factors that, over time, has accounted for the difference.

But political responsibility is not a question of revenge. I think victimization, or the sense of victimization, produces revenge. Criminal trials can be a substitute for people feeling that they need to take revenge. This, I think, is very important.

Just to cite one example in this connection: One of the places where terrible crimes took place in the post-World War II era was in Argentina during military rule from 1976 to 1983. An Argentine colleague points out that, despite the enormous number of killings and the known identities of the killers, there is actually not a single case of revenge that is known to have taken place subsequent to that period. Of course, there were trials of the persons principally responsible for what transpired in Argentina. The people who were convicted in those trials were eventually pardoned, but nevertheless there were trials. My friend believes that these trials helped to avoid revenge from being taken in Argentina. I also think that Argentina is a country that has developed a sense of political responsibility for the crimes that took place during the period of military rule. So, it may be that in some places, it takes some time after these crimes are committed for a sense of political responsibility to develop.

Samantha Power: In the United States, what I have been struck by—and I think you're seeing it in the debate about the International Criminal Court—is the extent to which military justice and accountability exist in their own special military province. We have our uniform military code. We have our mechanism for looking into war crimes. Military accountability is completely immune to legislative or even executive accountability.

Evidence supporting this point, which is almost more cultural than institutional, was revealed last year when the Bob Kerrey scandal broke. There were two accounts of what might have gone on in the Vietnamese village in question. One account described a free-fire zone; the other described the systematic murder of civilians at point-blank range. And the mere attempt to revisit these two scenarios created a virulent reaction: The issue has been investigated. What more do you want from us? What was amazing was not that this would be the military's position or former Senator Kerrey's position. Alleged perpetrators of war crimes tend to say, "I didn't do it." What was amazing was the way in which none of the institutions you would expect to press the issue—the journalists, the editorial boards, the Congress, the specific congressional committees—pressed it. None of them. There was a muteness that is partly specific to Vietnam, as if we've made our peace with Vietnam, agreeing to disagree and burying it and moving forward.

But this muzzling was also attributable to an idea that the military takes care of these matters itself. I can't even think of an example where external bodies have weighed in. This brings us back to Fred's point about political pressure and to Aryeh's point about victimization. Our sense of victimization after Somalia was such that to look at us as being in any way responsible for atrocities would have been hard to imagine from a political standpoint.

All of this points to the necessity to build constituencies on the outside that will press the issue. It will only work that way.

Tribunals: Imposing Responsibility, Imprisoning Criminals

Judge Patricia Wald: I have just returned after two years serving as the American judge on the Yugoslav tribunal. So my comments will be based primarily upon this experience. I, too, was intrigued by the title of this panel and its focus on different notions of responsibility. After my two years in The Hague, I am very much in favor of the tribunals. I'm also in favor of the International Criminal Court. And I am sorry the United States has not yet seen fit to join. I don't see any prospect of this happening in the immediate future. But I am enough of an optimist to hope that, if the ICC gets off to a good start and actually performs well, the United States will look at it after a number of years and that we may yet end up in it.

I've been in Washington the last six months. I have appeared before Congressional committees and before a number of symposia on which legislative people, sometimes the representatives themselves, sometimes their legislative aides, have also appeared. Several of them have remarked about the intensity of the opposition to the United States joining the ICC. An aide to Representative Tom Lantos, a member of one of these committees, said that, in all of his 20 years on the Hill, he had never encountered anything quite like the depth or the intensity of the opposition that the ICC has received. Other people, too, have suggested there is something else beneath many of the formal arguments in opposition to the ICC in the United States. Not just the military people, but also the politicians, feel it would be anathema for our conduct of a war or an intervention to be examined by other countries through a lens that allows them to feel free to make judgments about our conduct, judgments that would have repercussions for individual leaders in the military or civil branches.

One of the unique things about the tribunals that we always have to keep in mind is that, unlike many other methods of trying to impose responsibility, they actually put people away. They put people in prison in systems that are not their own, perhaps even to the end of their lives. The notion that any of our leaders or any of our servicemen could actually be put away in jail in some foreign country sends at least the political people in Washington into emotional orbit. It is pointed out again and again that most debates in Washington are not entirely rational. Of course, anytime that Americans go abroad and commit crimes on foreign soil they can be tried by foreign governments. And they are. Some of our soldiers are being tried now in Japan for rape in Okinawa. They are being tried in Japanese courts, according to Japanese rules of procedure. But somehow this just doesn't translate over into the notion that an international court could do the same thing.

Anyway, I do feel that there is a definite place for some kind of criminal-justice accountability after armed conflicts, whether the mechanism is international or national. But I also came away from my two years in The Hague with a strong question in my mind. It is a question to which the prior speakers have alluded. This question is: How far down the ladder do you go? How far down the ladder does it make sense to go using the tribunal mechanism? Whether or not it's a purely international tribunal like the ICTY or the Rwanda tribunal, or one of the new hybrid types, the mixed national and international courts that have more members from the national judiciary, as in East Timor, Sierra Leone, and some international examples. How far does it make sense to go down the line?

This brings up the whole notion of the involvement of thousands, perhaps tens of thousands of people or more, who, while they may not have actively committed any war crimes, were passive, complicit in these war crimes, in these terrible things that happened. Apart from the fact that most of these international tribunals simply don't have the resources to go too far down the line, the Rwanda tribunal even more than the Yugoslav tribunal has been criticized for the slowness of its trials, for their expense. During the two trials I participated in, we went back and forth, a couple of weeks on one trial, a couple weeks on the other, and they took up the entire two years I was there. I did work on some appeals; but these were extra time. If you do the trials well, they take a long time. This is not to say there aren't some efficiencies that could be implemented, there are. But, apart from the resource question, to me there's a real moral, conceptual problem about, for instance, Srebrenica.

I participated in a trial involving Srebrenica. We heard lots of testimony about what happened along the roads when they were busing the 25,000 to 30,000 women and children and elderly from Srebrenica—and keeping the men separate for ultimate execution. The soldiers were jeering at the buses. They were standing at the sides of the roads giving the Serb salute, or whatever it was, as these women and children were being bused out of the territory into Muslim-held territory. They were throwing stones at the buses. Well, these aren't war crimes. They don't rise to that level. But they certainly show a level of participation. After having been worked up by the nationalist leaders, the people were willing to go along.

But even more troubling to me was the question raised in the second case I had, the case involving the Omarska prison camp. The Omarska prison camp was one of the first prison camps to be exposed, and people immediately identified its victims with concentration camp victims from earlier times. The trial we had was of five men who were prison officials in the Omarska prison camp. Now, in one sense, the same situation prevailed as in Srebrenica. We did not have the man whom everybody recognized to be the main culprit, Ratko Mladic, the commander in chief of the Bosnian Serbs. General Radislav Krstic, the defendant before us, was one level below him.

Now, in the Omarska case, the commandant of the prison camp was indicted but never arrested. He simply got away. So what you had was one deputy commander who was there for three or four weeks, two shift commanders, and one person who, it was unclear exactly, did a lot of paperwork around the camp. Now we had evidence that only one or two of the five people before us had actively participated, personally, in the war crimes. These two were like the earlier case, the Tadic case, where a person committed brutal acts upon others. There was no evidence that the other three people had ever laid hands on any of the prisoners. In fact, there was a question as to whether or not they brought food to the prisoners from a neighbor or from the families. And there was certainly no evidence that they had ever ordered any kind of brutality to be employed upon the prisoners.

So, the real issue involved the kind of ultimate question raised by Dante's *Inferno*: Is the hottest part of hell reserved for those who stand by and let terrible things happen? This is very interesting rhetorically. Does it comport with the levels of criminal responsibility that we want to impose, or should impose, upon people who become involved in these activities? I'm not giving you a yes or a no answer. We did find these people guilty, and the case is now on appeal. But we found them guilty on a theory of involvement in a criminal enterprise that goes back to Nuremberg and the concentration camp cases, mainly the death camp cases. The Nuremberg trials said that if people went into a death camp knowing that extermination was the be-all and end-all of the camp, then even a cook or somebody who just guarded the perimeter was participating in a criminal enterprise. It didn't matter whether or not their particular roles involved doing something that was itself illegal.

On the other hand, Nuremberg also had different kinds of precedents. You can go through the Nuremberg cases and find different reasoning and sometimes even different results from one case to another. But these present-day cases, many of which are still being tried in the Yugoslav tribunal and perhaps in the Rwanda tribunal, raise the question of how far down the line you go for criminal responsibility. Interestingly enough, a lot of the same kinds of people and groups who get very excited and protective—justifiably so—about the standards for criminal responsibility and for criminal procedure in the case of defendants in the United States, are more concerned about the victims of war crimes abroad. In most of these cases, the criminal rights that you normally worry about for defendants in the United States are ones that involve the alleged perpetrators of war crimes abroad. So how far down the line do you want to apply criminal responsibility for people who were more passively involved in these massive war crimes? And how far do you want to go to make international criminal procedure more lenient than say American or Anglo-Saxon criminal procedure when you're trying these people.

Command Responsibility: When Did He Know? What Did He Do?

Many, many things in an international tribunal would raise eyebrows in an American court. You have to think very carefully about the whole notion of what we and the European Commission on Human Rights and the European Court in Strasbourg have always stood up for regarding the necessary protections in criminal law and the whole notion of how far down the line you go with imputed criminal responsibility. This will continue to come up again and again in the cases of the leaders sitting in their offices, in Belgrade or in the field headquarters. For example, during the entire week the executions were taking place in Srebrenica, General Krstic was up in Zepa waging a military campaign. So, with him there were two questions. When did he become commander? And, once he became commander, did he know that the executions were taking place down the line where Mladic was on the ground? And did he then not do anything about it?

These questions come up again and again. If we're to believe the newspapers in the United States, the Justice Department is looking closely at using a form of criminal enterprise or conspiracy theory to go after the members of Al Qaeda. This could raise some similar questions. We have a different legal tradition domestically. In a case involving the Communist Party, the Supreme Court was reasonably strict in saying that just becoming a member of the Party was not enough for a person to be tried for violent acts committed by other Party members. The question of the kind of law we're making in the tribunals in order to get at people we think are really bad and how much of this law could in turn be used in other situations is one that we have to worry about.

The second point that I'm going to raise and speak to very briefly is the role of tribunals in history, in making history. This has bothered me a great deal. One of the justifications for the tribunal, apart from the purely criminal-justice, accountability factor, is to document some of these terrible things that have happened. And this is fine. But I think there are often problems. If you are making history in an adversarial criminal process, it may not be the same kind of history that either you or some historian would write at a later date. At the ICTY there are at least four prosecutions, either in process or completed, that center on one attack by Bosnian Croats on the small village of Ahmici in central Bosnia. Why are four prosecutions necessary? It is part of the whole tribunal business. They catch people at different times, and then have to start a prosecution within a reasonable time. The prosecutors can't say, "Well, you've got to sit here for eight years until we see if we can find all the other people involved."

So they start. Two and a half years later, they catch somebody else involved in the same incident. In the meantime, more evidence may have become available about what happened because, as Croatia and even Serbia have become slightly more friendly to the tribunals, they're more open with the evidence in their archives. Evidence is now pouring out of the Croatian archives, and this evidence may change facts that were found in old cases. You may get different accounts. It is a matter of judgment how important the differences are—the differences having to do with who were the prime leaders of the attack.

The one example I want to give springs from Srebrenica. At the end of the 98 days of testimony, the judges are allowed by the rules to call their own witnesses, which is somewhat different from our American procedure but not unheard of in other countries. So the three judges on our panel said, "Well, we've heard from hundreds of victims who were there. We've heard from Dutch soldiers. We've heard from some of the UN observers in Potocari. We've heard through the defense from Bosnian Serb people who were in the Bosnian Serb army at the time. But we haven't had a single witness from the Muslim army." Part of the Muslim army, the 28th Division, was in Srebrenica and on the outskirts or in Tuzla helping to get some of the fighters or some of the people trying to flee Srebrenica onto Muslim-held territory. "Well, you know, why haven't we heard from anyone about that side of the story?" So the court, in its naiveté, said, "We want to hear." We knew who they were. Some had written books about their experiences. So, the two relevant generals were called. They agreed to come, and they said they did not want any protection or safe passage. One of them was an acting minister in the present Bosnian Federation government. So they came. Their testimony did not turn out to be absolutely crucial, but we used parts of it in our fact-finding missions. We noticed that the prosecution never asked them a single question, even though the prosecution and the defense both had that right.

The day after the judgment in our Srebrenica case was issued, the prosecutors published their indictment of one of those Muslim generals for incidents that had nothing to do with Srebrenica, a completely different crime. Two weeks later, they indicted the other one. They had these simultaneous tracks of prosecution and didn't want to hurt their cases by getting involved in having those generals come to The Hague to testify.

I'm not saying that somehow we didn't get all the facts straight. I'm saying there are problems with relying upon tribunals in an adversary process to give you the absolutely full account of what happened. I think they can give you parts. They can probably be very helpful in this way. Right now there is a *Washington Post* reporter who is resisting a subpoena, a binding order, to testify in one of the trials. There is a big question about whether or not the reporters and the press feel it will decrease their ability to get their truth out from the scene if it's felt that eventually they may be called as a witness.

The victimization issue has been discussed by prior speakers in terms of people feeling they were actually victims when they acted, when they were committing "war crimes." I would like to say that, from the point of view of the court, many of the defendants felt that they were victims when they were in the dock. All of the defendants in the cases I had were Bosnian Serbs. They felt that the Balkans had been picked on with this tribunal. The judges came from America, Egypt, China. In some of their defense arguments, they would raise the point that the judges were representatives of countries whose human rights records were, if anything, worse than their country's and ask why had they been plucked out. I have always thought an international criminal court with global jurisdiction would at least take care of this problem. Although it wouldn't try every crime that came to its attention, it would be making choices based upon the total pool that was before them rather than on one in particular.

The second aspect of victimization arises when some mid-level person on trial picks up the paper and reads that the top-level guy has gone to a soccer game in Belgrade. Or the mid-level person who only carried papers and called out names finds that he is going to be convicted on a criminal-enterprise theory while the commander of the camp has managed to avoid arrest and is walking around free.

The last war story I'll tell involves the first case in the tribunal's history, in which an appellate tribunal overturned the convictions of one of the trial panels. We overturned the convictions of three Bosnian Croats on grounds familiar to people in the U.S. court system: the evidence just wasn't sufficient to come up to the level of "beyond a reasonable doubt." Okay. So these three Croats went back to their village, Ahmici, again. A Dutch newspaper reporter wrote that they weren't bitter and that they were going to try to seek reconciliation. Another reporter who visited Ahmici recently told me that there were conspiracy theories all over the place. The Bosnian Croats felt that the case showed that all the prosecutions of Bosnian Croats in the area were really a big conspiracy to get them. The Muslims, of course, who were the victims at Ahmici, were completely unhappy with the reversals of the Croats' convictions.

This brings up another point that ought to be looked at in future tribunals. While I think the effect of accountability, even in the criminal area and certainly for top people, is very positive, I don't think this always gets communicated to the public. Just showing the ICTY trials on television in the Balkans is not enough. Most ordinary people, sitting there watching three judges and a witness testifying, don't get the full importance of it. The reporter said the people in Ahmici really don't understand why the convictions were overturned. Neither side understands really what the case stood for, why it happened, whether it was a technical error or a fundamental injustice.

What happens in the tribunal is very hard to disseminate to people, because judges, even international judges, tend to carry over the same practices we have as domestic judges and never talk to the newspapers. You know you should never try to explain anything that went on in the courtroom, even after the trial is all over. Half the time I think the press doesn't fully understand what is sometimes a 200-page judgment. I don't blame them. The reporters used to run down to the lobby in the ICTY to a friend of mine at an NGO and ask, "What does this mean? What does this mean? Can you tell us? We have to get the story out tomorrow. Could you just tell us in a couple of sentences, what does this mean?" So, it's not always possible for them to get a meaningful account out either.

I'm not sure that there isn't a big gap between what the tribunals are seeking to accomplish, what they do accomplish, and what actually gets transmitted down on the ground. All that said, however, I still think the tribunals serve a very noble purpose. But you cannot lay too much on them. I don't think they are the sole answer to the problem of war crimes. I think some of these other mechanisms, like truth-and-reconciliation commissions, compensation, and other types of processes, have to be explored as well.

Selective Prosecution: Who Is Indicted, Who Isn't

Fred Abrahams: I want, first of all, to touch on the notion of how far down the chain you go. I want to suggest another way to phrase this. It is not how far "down" you go, because the word "down" suggests a vertical hierarchy. The problem involves decisions that are made in general.

I would also like to comment on institutional momentum. Once an institution like the ICTY is created, it comes under tremendous public and political pressure to show results. And this, in my opinion, had an impact on the ICTY that was not always positive in terms of the decisions that were made. The best example I can give involves people who are not indicted, or at least not publicly indicted. Some of these I consider to be critical actors, at least regarding Kosovo, which is the area I'm most familiar with.

Take the case of the minister of interior, Vlajko Stojiljkovic, who killed himself on the steps of the Parliament in Belgrade a few weeks ago. He had been indicted along with Milosevic. Many people, most Serbs among them, believe that Stojiljkovic was a Milosevic crony, a rubber stamp. On the other hand, there are still no indictments of key architects in the secret service and the organizers of the paramilitary units, people like Frenki Simatovic, who ran the notorious "Frenki's Boys," or the head of that unit, Milorad Ulemek, known as Legija. These are key people in the structure. Another issue is the difference between the de facto and de jure chains of command within the structures. Things so often did not function under a clear legal mechanism. The point that I'm making is that there are certain pressures to go after the people that everybody knows while key actors remain unaffected.

The other point that Judge Wald raised is about truth and history. I agree that the full story of these complicated events cannot emerge through a criminal proceeding. But I am also a strong proponent of attempting to tell as complete a story as possible. So, accepting the fact that the proceedings will not tell the whole story and that it will require historians and journalists and ongoing research, the persons conducting the proceedings should nevertheless endeavor to build as complete an account as possible. Perhaps there's a legal limitation, because you have to set the context of the crime. But I would hope they try to tell the full story. For example, I think it is relevant to examine the revocation of Kosovo's autonomy and the discrimination in the early 1990s that preceded the crimes a defendant is accused of committing in 1999.

Lastly, I would like to touch on the impact the tribunal is having on the ground. The tribunal did not do an adequate job of informing people. Indictments were not available in the local language, and people did not have full information about what was happening. This led to confusion, speculation, and rumor. I believe that the tribunal has gotten much better at outreach. But there was a tendency to focus on the courtroom and on Holland. There wasn't enough attention paid to how people were receiving information about and interpreting these dramatic events.

Judge Patricia Wald: I agree with you. I know the outreach program. And I am all for it. In fact, all three judges on my tribunal went to Croatia. We spoke with judges and prosecutors there. Other people did this in Bosnia. We could not go in there, however, and explain how we reached a certain verdict in a certain way. This is anathema to any judge in any system.

I campaigned, to some degree unsuccessfully, to get more readable and shorter judgments. These 200- and 300-page documents, while they do serve the purpose of recording the factual elements that you're talking about, are too taken up by the fact-finding. They are not easy reading even for people who write law review articles. And the people of Ahmici do not read law review articles. The only thing they know is that these three neighbors who had been in jail for four years in The Hague suddenly flew in on a plane and reappeared one night in their village to be greeted by cheering crowds.

I don't know what the answer is. But it does seem to me there should be some interpretative vehicle that attempts to explain the cases and decisions to them. Interestingly enough, a Dutch newspaper interviewed the prosecutor in the very case reversed on appeal, one of the first prosecutions brought in 1995. The prosecutor, who was French, said, "I don't think we ever should have brought those prosecutions. The pressure was so great at the time. I don't think these prosecutions would have been brought in France or in Holland."

So your comments about institutional momentum bring us back to the debate on the special prosecutor in the United States and, you know, the "if-you-build-it, they-will-come" kind of thing. I did not come away with the general impression that there were untoward prosecutions in The Hague. And God knows that I've reversed a lot of convictions in the United States from district courts, too. So it's not an unusual occurrence. But people would be mistaken to think that just by bringing these proceedings before a tribunal—be it an international tribunal or a hybrid tribunal—they're suddenly getting rid of all of the normal, what I call, internal system politics. This is not politics in which somebody calls you up and says decide the outcome in a certain way. But the pressure on the prosecutor to get indictments out and other kinds of internal institutional pressures figure into which cases are brought and which cases are not brought.

Telling History: The Credibility of Cross-Examination

Aryeh Neier: One word in defense of the tribunals in the telling of history. With all of the inadequacies, it did seem to me that Nuremberg had value because the defendants were represented by defense counsel. And this defense counsel had an opportunity to cross-examine witnesses, introduce witnesses, and present evidence. If you think of the different ways in which history can be told, the criminal trial is unique in allowing the adversarial process to take place. It allows the accused the opportunity to rebut the accusations. It has, in this respect, a certain kind of credibility. It is another matter whether this credibility is being achieved at the same moment as the trial or whether the credibility is achieved many years later, when there is a revisionist attempt to tell the story. But, there is no other historical form that I can think of that allows this kind of rebuttal to take place.

Judge Patricia Wald: Telford Taylor, when he was writing *The Anatomy of the Nuremberg Trials*, made this point himself. The Nuremberg charter stated that they had to admit all of the written factual depositions from the Russian commissions and commissions set up by the victims in some of the occupied countries. There were thousands and thousands of them. Taylor commented somewhat skeptically on their credibility. He was not sure whether or not every last jot of evidence in these reports was true, and I don't think it's the best way to get evidence either. Overall, however, I don't think it's a bad thing to take evidence on historical events. But, you know, he had some questions about its accuracy, and I do too.

Chief Prosecutor at Nuremberg Robert H. Jackson's famous comment, which I quoted again and again over there, was that we must establish incredible events by credible evidence. And so there's that whole extra debate about what the laws of evidence should be in these international tribunals. But, I agree, we cannot fail to find the facts and we should try to do the best job we can. Yet we should keep in mind that it may not be the final telling or the last word, especially when you have Balkan defense lawyers who have never cross-examined witnesses before in their lives. It isn't part of their tradition. The tribunal holds training courses for them; but cross-examination is the kind of thing that you learn in the first year of law school in an Anglo-Saxon environment where it is so much part of the adversarial process. It's not so easy to learn on the run in a courtroom. And I thought some of the cross-examination was pretty feeble.

Dinah PoKempner: I'd also like to disagree with you, Aryeh. I think a trial is a good method of generating history. But it is a very incomplete one. This is particularly true with respect to the defendant's story. What the defendant will want to say is overwhelmed by the context of facing a legal consequence. I think that there is a possibility of getting perpetrators to speak after the events and after the moment of justice as well.

During my recent travels in Cambodia, I was struck by the high expectations of ordinary people that a tribunal would tell this story and answer the question, "Why did they do it?" And yet, how unlikely a trial would be to answer any of the dimensions of this question. This is not to say a tribunal wouldn't be important. But we're talking about how to engage a sense of social responsibility. Samantha and Fred and many others have said it is the sense of social responsibility that can impel action or act as a check. And I don't think that trials will necessarily do that.

Joost Hiltermann: I might as well move into a critique of the human rights movement. What I found working for human rights organizations is that the tradition is really to interview victims and to build a story on the basis of testimonies taken from witnesses who are mostly on the receiving end of the violence, including refugees and others. And because it is so difficult, there is very little attempt to interview the perpetrators and to get them on record.

Documents, when available, are extremely helpful, because they can be incriminating. In the Iraqi case, for example, we have 18 metric tons of secret-police documents. They very clearly lay out the case that Iraq was guilty of very serious crimes. But this kind of access to documents is just not the case in many situations.

One particularly interesting subgroup that drew our attention when I was at Human Rights Watch were the "disenchanted perpetrators," the persons who have pangs of conscience after the fact or who, for political reasons, have parted ways with their former comrades in arms. For a Human Rights Watch report on violence in Kenya in 1997, we interviewed so-called raiders who had become disenchanted afterwards, because, for a number of reasons, they had become outcasts. They gave detailed testimony, explaining their motivations and the intentions behind the attacks. It was extremely useful testimony that rounded out the picture we wouldn't have gotten simply by interviewing the witnesses. In trials you often get the perpetrators. But again it's in different circumstances. I would strongly encourage human rights organizations in particular to also go after the perpetrators.

Aryeh Neier: I was going to comment on this question of documents, because at Nuremberg, of course, there was a vast amount of documentary evidence available. In the case of the court for the former Yugoslavia, there is very little in the way of documentary evidence. This suggests to me that the telling of the history through the trials takes on an increased importance.

Think of the other ways of telling history. Historians tend to rely a great deal on documents, and the absence of documents in the case of the former Yugoslavia is going to hamper the historical enterprise significantly. Thus far, we have three main ways of knowing the history of the former Yugoslavia. The first is through journalism, because journalists went to the scenes where things happened and they interviewed participants. The second is through the trials, because prosecutors and investigators interview participants and take testimony. And the third is through human rights reporting, which is also an interviewing technique. I suspect that it's likely to remain this way and that there isn't going to be a great deal of important historical writing on the former Yugoslavia, because of the lack of documents.

Tribunals: The Value of Demystifying Ethnic Conflicts

Bill Berkeley: I agree with most of what has been said about both the inadequacies of trials as historical narratives and the importance of them. But one of the most valuable services performed by some of these tribunals is their ability to demystify ethnic conflict. Most of us would agree, certainly most of us in the United States, that the perception of ethnic conflict is that it is some sort of mysterious phenomenon growing out of ancient hatreds. Recall President Clinton's speech at the time of the Kosovo conflict in which he acknowledged, some six or seven years into his presidency, that he had misunderstood the roots of ethnic conflict in the Balkans. This is the leader of the free world reflecting, I think, the perception of his people and his nation. I think trials contribute to an understanding that these are not mysterious conflicts. To the extent that trials document the roles of individual leaders and the dynamics of these conflicts, they can demystify them.

It is certainly the case that the misperception of ancient hatreds in Africa is much more deeply rooted. Trials, I can speak for myself, provide the fodder for writers and historians, the evidentiary basis for writing historical narratives that illuminate the dynamics of these conflicts. I covered the Rwanda tribunal's first complete trial, the trial of Jean-Paul Akayesu, a small-time mayor convicted of genocide in 1998 and also of rape as a component crime of genocide. His trial was significant if for no other reason than it established rape as a component crime of genocide. But it also illuminated the dynamics of mass slaughter in Rwanda and the importance of hierarchy in a culture of obedience in Rwanda. This was a small-time mayor who had no history of racism, no history of criminality, but who, for apparently opportunistic reasons, made a political calculation that it was in his interest to go along with the genocide. Shortly thereafter, all of his constituents joined in the killing.

So, I think that trials, as a means of demystifying ethnic conflict, have a value in themselves.

It is difficult to answer the question how far down the hierarchy prosecutions need to go. I don't necessarily have an answer. This is a question that Africans themselves were asking even as the killing was going on in Rwanda. I want to quote a conversation that I had with a couple of Rwandan Tutsis in Rwanda in June of 1994 while the killing was still going on. Both of them had lost many relatives in the killings. I interviewed the two men, Bonaventure and Isadore, as internal refugees in a bombed-out, looted village in Rwanda. I asked them how Rwanda could possibly overcome the disaster of the genocide. Bonaventure replied, "There is only one way, and that is to find the people who have been responsible for this and bring them to trial according to the law."

Isadore agreed, abruptly revising his theory about illiteracy. (Initially he thought the reason people were killing each other was because they were illiterate. I had pointed out that the Germans were among the best-educated people on Earth during the Holocaust.) He drew up a list of those he would bring to trial. At the top was Colonel Theoneste Bagosora, the notorious defense chief, widely viewed as the mastermind behind the genocide. He scribbled more names. "They were educated people," he explained: "the administrative chain of command from the president on down, the prefects, the governors, the mayors. They were galvanizing the killers."

I asked Isadore if he would bring his neighbors to trial, the ones he thought were his friends. He thought for a moment and shook his head. "To me, they are just instruments," he said. "If you bring these people to justice, you'll take everybody. It'll be an endless process. But if the people at the top are punished according to the law and the population knows that, that is the only way."

Bonaventure vehemently disagreed. "People who have murdered have to be punished," he said. "The level of responsibility is not the same. But you cannot say this person who took a machete and killed this baby, that he is not responsible. He must be responsible for his acts, ignorance is no defense." So, these are two Rwandan Tutsis, while the genocide was still going on, having exactly the same debate.

István Rév, director, Open Society Archives: There is a real temptation to write history by legal means. Modern historical writing did not originate with the Greeks, but with the monks in Western Europe's monasteries in the 11th and 12th centuries. And as a result, the historical enterprise was completely mixed up with legal reasoning. The monks were trying to keep their property. They forged donation letters, or tried to find the donation letters that were still available. And they wrote history in order to prove in court that the property rightfully belonged to their monasteries.

There are other reasons why it is so tempting to try to write history by legal means. First, the narrative has no subjective known author. Although we know the names of the judges who write the opinion in a case, the author of the legal opinion and the legal document at the end is the court and not X or Y. It seems to be that it is not subjective, unlike history writing. There is a closure, the sentence at the very end of the procedure, and it seems to justify the story. There is an inherent justification inside the story itself, which is lacking in the case of an historical narrative.

I think, however, that there should be a division of labor between historians and lawyers and judges. In the case of Nuremberg, there was more or less a story in place even before the trials. This is not the story we know today about the responsibility of the Germans and the history of World War II. The story at that time was that the Germans were indeed responsible, but the story's centerpiece was their waging a war of aggression, not their perpetrating the Holocaust. That was a different story. When the Nuremberg trials took place, there was no real Germany. There were no real German citizens anymore. So the nonexistent citizens of this nonexistent country were solely responsible for the Second World War. All the defendants of the main Nuremberg trial were former German citizens, and all the others were able to claim that they were simply victims.

The story that had been constructed before the end of the war was then justified during the Nuremberg trials and it worked well for a while. I don't think that what happened subsequently in Germany, especially after the Frankfurt trial and the Eichmann trial, which played a major role in the German historical debates, was the direct continuation of the Nuremberg trials. I don't want to deny that the Nuremberg trials played a role later on in the new debates. But there was no direct continuation between the two.

Legal reasoning is different from historical reasoning. In order to be able to bring somebody to court, you have to reconstruct the story, sometimes in dramatically different ways.

In Hungary, for example, one of the first ambitions of the post-communist government was to try to bring to court the perpetrators of the post-1956 terror and the people who were responsible for the massacres in the course of the revolution. But more than three decades had already passed. The only possibility seemed to be to try people on the basis of the Geneva Conventions. It was necessary then to prove that members of the police or regular army killed peaceful civilians in the days of 1956. The government assigned a department in the Ministry of Justice to come up with a story. The story they concocted said that armed people did not try to storm the Hungarian National Radio on the first day of the revolution. The members of the secret police did not shoot at storming revolutionaries, but rather at peaceful passers-by who were walking in the streets in front of the radio station. The hope was that it would be possible to try the perpetrators on the basis of this story. So, the legal requirement in this case was to prove that there was no revolution in 1956 in order to be able legally to try the people who were responsible for defeating the 1956 revolution.

This is an extreme example. But there are similar cases in which the requirements of due legal procedure are completely different from what should be necessary for a historian to write the history of a certain event.

Going after the Big Fish, Relieving Society of Responsibility

Dinah PoKempner: The question of how far down the line does it makes sense to go is very interesting. I've mentioned how difficult it is to actually make cases against the big fish. Judge Wald mentioned that there's an element of moral ambivalence as well. How far do you want to expand legal doctrine to encompass these crimes of omission, or willful ignorance, or negligent ignorance?

In Cambodia, these same debates are going on. And there's huge resistance to going down the line. There's a lot of support for keeping it to the big fish, because once you go down the line, it feels like half the country could be prosecuted. This would bring up the issue of renewing civil war. But a problem with going after the big fish to show that they're responsible is that in a sense it relieves the rest of society of responsibility. There is the wishful thinking that, well, the higher-ups were guilty, and we were following them, and we couldn't have done anything about it.

Maybe this problem will be solved during the second or third generation after the fact. Every history develops. Every history has its revisionism. And I think trials are exposed to revisionism as well as they become historical facts and are reinterpreted and reargued throughout the generations.

How do you use the criminal process to engage social responsibility rather than bury it? This is a really serious problem. I don't think we've really grappled with it well. The gap that Judge Wald was talking about in translating legal conclusions, or legal decisions, into something that makes popular sense is a gap because of values. Every trial, you know, is a unique story, but all trials have similar story components. All trials tell us about certain legal values, certain rule-of-law values, like procedural fairness. Criminal trials tell us about the unwillingness to impose punishment unless it is merited beyond a reasonable doubt. This is a very high standard. It is not a populist concept. Failure to prove guilt "beyond a reasonable doubt" means you know a defendant might have been doing bad things but that it is possible to have doubts. The state hasn't carried its burden, which isn't to say that a better prosecutor couldn't have done it. In some legal systems, there are intermediate ways of assigning responsibility that carry consequences. For example, civil liability doesn't have to be beyond a reasonable doubt. It can be just a probability. The consequences that come out of a civil liability–apart from a public statement of liability, a governmental statement of responsibility, which is very important–include reparations. Often this is as important to victims and as effective a deterrent as imprisonment.

In the international context, we haven't really figured out how to provide gradations of responsibility. The reparations issue is married to the criminal trial. We don't have an international court of civil liability. There are, perhaps, other mechanisms. To some degree, truth commissions and historical commissions do carry real consequences, if not criminal consequences, that are meaningful and helpful. But there is a lot of skepticism in the human rights community about these commissions. They could become excuses for avoiding the question of criminal responsibility. And the consequences that these commissions carry, the kind of social stigmatization they create, are not as meaningful as criminal stigmatization.

One of the key issues is to be able to engage society. You have to be able to speak not just to legal values and to translate them well. You have to be able to speak to other social values that provide a will to justice and a will to resist injustice. You have to call on the kinds of values that would make the bystanders, the society itself, willing to challenge injustice.

Right now, for example, there is an attempt on the part of intellectuals to draw out of Cambodian history examples of resistance to authority. This is a very unlikely endeavor, I have to say, because until now resistance is a completely undiscovered cultural theme. But some intellectuals are nevertheless making strenuous efforts to draw out, for example, the willingness of rulers to subject themselves to the law or to limit their actions. They are striving to draw out the importance of women and their independent authority. These are all themes that are so counter to how most Cambodians see their culture that it's striking that people are even trying. I think the most creative people are seeking an alternative source of values and resistance, because the legal values only go so far in terms of popular engagement.

Joost Hiltermann: Among perpetrators, there is great reluctance–and partly, I think, it is deliberate–to distinguish between the justness of a cause and the means used in accomplishing it. The recent case of Israeli forces in Jenin is telling. The Israeli authorities did not want a UN fact-finding mission to go into Jenin. They said that their cause was just and that they were going after legitimate targets. What they didn't want to acknowledge, however, was that, in the process of going after legitimate targets, they might have used excessive force and, in fact, committed crimes of war. These are the means used. And the problem is that the justness of a cause can be undermined by the illegitimacy of the means used. The more illegitimate the means, the more the justness of the cause is eroded.

This, of course, is also true for interventions in humanitarian crises where the cause is just. This is why they're called humanitarian interventions. But when the humanitarian intervention ends up with the intervening forces violating human rights, then immediately there is criticism and the very enterprise of these humanitarian interventions is on the line.

Witnesses to War Crimes: Who Gets Immunity from Testifying?

David Rohde: I would like to ask Judge Wald about the case involving the *Washington Post* reporter. I wasn't aware of it.

Judge Patricia Wald: Another lawyer told me about it. So it is hearsay. But I trust the lawyer. I don't think the case has been decided. I believe there is a *Washington Post* reporter who was subpoenaed by the prosecution, because he had interviewed one of the defendants, the accused, at the time of the event. The question now is whether or not he should have immunity because of his position as a journalist. I think the question has already been decided in favor of immunity from testifying for humanitarian aid workers and UN workers. I don't know of any decision yet by the tribunal. But I know it's a question being briefed and argued. In fact, Richard Goldstone, in the preface to *Crimes of War*, the Roy Gutman book, takes up the issue, declaring himself in favor of such immunity for reporters.

Aryeh Neier: I can recall paying a visit in 1993 to the headquarters of the International Committee of the Red Cross in Geneva to talk to top ICRC officials about whether they would be willing to testify before the Yugoslavia tribunal because the ICRC is present at the scene when many things take place. One of the practices of the International Committee of the Red Cross is to inform commanders that war crimes are being committed. They do so on a confidential basis. But it seemed to me that this might be very valuable evidence for the tribunal because it would be a way of demonstrating knowledge by commanders of the crimes that were being committed. The particular officials I spoke to were extremely nervous about testifying. The International Committee of the Red Cross gets access to a lot of places precisely on the basis that it will maintain confidentiality—other than to inform commanders of crimes. Its access depends on this confidentiality. Something of a debate took place within the ICRC as to what its posture should be. At one point they issued a statement saying that those persons responsible for war crimes should not count on the ICRC to maintain confidentiality in such circumstances. Nevertheless, to my knowledge, none of their officials has actually been called to testify.

Dinah PoKempner: To the contrary, they took a position asserting a privilege. And they were upheld at the trial level. But my understanding is that the prosecutor's office did not decide to appeal it for the moment, because they may want to appeal it at another time. The case did not involve calling an acting ICRC official, but a former employee who, voluntarily, wished to come forward to testify. It's a very difficult issue. But I guess I've made my position clear. I think we really ought to consider whether there is a moral responsibility. The trial court attempted to find some customary international-law privilege, given the historic role of the ICRC with respect to the laws of war. In the case of other kinds of witnesses, I don't know if the courts are going to find some customary international-law privilege. There certainly isn't one in the statute.

István Rév: The International Committee of the Red Cross is even more cautious than that. Originally there was a plan to deposit the Physicians for Human Rights Bosnia Project documents in Geneva at the archives of the ICRC. But when it became evident to the Red Cross that there was a chance that the tribunal in The Hague might decide to look into these documents, which the ICRC had nothing to do with obtaining, they decided they did not want them. It was too dangerous for them. So this is how the whole collection came to the Open Society Archives here in Budapest.

Returning to your remark about the unavailability of documents about Yugoslavia, you are absolutely right. But there are very important indirect documents. As you know, we monitored the news in Belgrade, Zagreb, and Sarajevo every day during the war. We have copies of the nightly news programs, which document how the war was represented by the different belligerent parties throughout the conflicts. Sometimes they were reckless enough to show certain incriminating acts caught on camera. So we have this very valuable documentation that will definitely be used by historians, if not by the court.

Judge Patricia Wald: In the Srebrenica trial, the question was at what point did General Krstic know that these things were going on. Physically, he was someplace else. He was in Zepa while the killings were going on in Srebrenica. And one of the pieces of evidence we did rely upon was the fact of news broadcasts around the world about the fall of Srebrenica. The killings had been broadcast on the news in certain places that week and certain people at the UN had said things about what was happening in that area. This kind of general knowledge can be very important, because the big question in command responsibility is whether the superior officer knew or had reason to know that these violations were being committed by the troops. It is usually the question of the time at which this knowledge came. None of the defendants that I know of say, "Oh, I knew that. I knew that." It's always: "I didn't know that." "I didn't hear about that until three weeks later." "I didn't hear about that until months later."

David Rohde: I was asked to testify at the Srebrenica trial and I did not. I drew a moral line at whether or not my testimony would be pivotal in deciding the outcome of the case. I understand the ICRC's hesitancy, and I think it's important for journalists not to be seen as an arm of the United States government or any war crimes tribunal. If we uncover information, we make it public. We are here to inform the public. We don't testify at Congressional hearings for that reason. And it is, unfortunately, increasingly dangerous to be a journalist. Maybe it's naive to think you'll be seen as unbiased if you don't testify at these trials. But I think it's very important to maintain that separation.

Fred, will you testify?

Fred Abrahams: I was going to raise this very question. Do we as human rights activists testify? We attempt to provide objective unbiased reporting in the same way that journalists do. But we decided that there was a contribution to make here. We supported the process enough to contribute to it and decided that testifying wouldn't undermine our credibility as objective observers. But we must discuss this. It's a relevant point.

Aryeh Neier: I don't think it's a closed question. A human rights group, on the one hand, has to be objective in terms of getting the facts right and being even-handed in its reporting. But, on the other hand, it is also an advocacy institution. It is trying to achieve a certain result. Part of the reason it is presenting its evidence is to contribute to the punishment of those who commit severe abuses of human rights. Presenting its evidence in court seems to me to be consistent with the mission of a human rights organization. By contrast, journalists don't represent themselves as advocates. They may, if they do things other than daily news reporting, engage in advocacy. For example, an editorial takes an advocacy stance. But you don't cover a conflict through the editorial process. You cover a conflict through the daily reporting process. So I would differentiate news reporting from human rights reporting. Objectivity is only one aspect of human rights reporting, whereas from the daily news-reporting standpoint, objectivity really is everything.

Bill Berkeley: If I could just put in my own two cents as a journalist and a one-time editorial writer. I was also asked to testify twice at the Rwanda tribunal, once in the Bagosora trial, and once in a trial that is now ongoing. I wrestled with it. I didn't find it an easy call—in part because the prosecutor argued that my testimony could actually swing a case.

I had written a story in 1994, while the massacres were still going on in Rwanda, about the radio propaganda. In the story, I quoted some of the killers. They explained why they were killing people. Their point was that they heard on the radio, the state-controlled radio, that the Tutsis were coming to kill them. The Tutsis were coming to re-impose feudalism. This was late in the genocide. It turned out to be a unique account in which the killers themselves acknowledged that it was the radio that had provoked them to kill. The prosecutors needed to link the propaganda to the killers. And they wanted me to testify to that effect. I was tempted to do so.

Soon after this appeal was made to me, however, I wound up writing editorials. I wrote a number about the Rwanda tribunal. I found that the possibility of my participating in the tribunal, even in a subjective sense, colored my analysis of what was going on in the tribunal. I felt that even as an editorial writer, it was very important for me to be detached vis-à-vis the institution itself, not just the crime or the perpetrators. Even though, as an editorial writer, I had an advocacy role, I still view it as fundamentally a journalistic role in which the inquiry needs to be detached. To the extent that I wanted to have credibility as an editorial writer, I felt it would be very important that I not be seen as an arm of the prosecution or as an arm of the institution. My colleagues at the time agreed with this, and so I declined.

Judge Patricia Wald: Can I just raise one possible distinction that, as a judge, might have bothered me. I didn't have a reporter problem in any of the trials I was involved with. I did have powerful video testimony. Some of the videos in Srebrenica were done by Serb people on the spot, which made them, if anything, a better tool for the prosecution, a powerful tool. But we did have this question come up with newspaper articles. Somebody would introduce a newspaper article about such and such a thing. And the defendant sometimes would say, "But that's not what I said. I didn't say that. I was misquoted in the paper." That happened in the Krstic trial. At one point he said of one of the audiotapes, "No, they doctored it. That's not my voice." In other words, the defendants deny outright the authenticity of either the article and the quote or the voice on the tape. Then the question comes up—you would normally go to the person who wrote the article or did the film and obtain authentication. I don't know whether your very understandable position with regard to reporters testifying would cover this kind of situation.

Bill Berkeley: Well, that was the reason why the prosecutor wanted me to travel all the way to Tanzania, to verify the quotes in case a defense lawyer raised objections on the ground that "Can anybody prove that this was actually an accurate quote? Can anybody prove that this was actually said?" They wanted the reporter on hand to testify about the veracity of his reporting.

Determining Guilt: Who Is Responsible?

Moderator: *Aryeh Neier*
Speaker: *David Rohde*
Comments: *G.M. Tamás*, visiting professor, Central European University

Aryeh Neier: David Rohde is going to speak about the subject of "Determining Guilt: Who Is Responsible?" G.M. Tamás will respond. Tamás, who has held a variety of academic appointments, was an intellectual leader of the democratic opposition during the period the Communist regime was still in power in Hungary.

The Attack on the Jenin Refugee Camp

David Rohde: I thought that Judge Wald did an excellent job of laying out the basic facts of what went on in Srebrenica and the unresolved issues that still surround it. I want to talk more about my recent reporting. These are all very rough impressions I've gathered from reporting in Israel and Afghanistan, and specifically I would like to talk about the Jenin refugee camp and the attack there. I think a lot of the same themes that were discussed are apparent in that event and in the reactions to it, in terms of the sense of victimization on both sides and also the lack of accountability.

The events in Jenin are in dispute. Journalists who got into the camp did some initial reporting. James Bennett, a colleague of mine at the *New York Times*, did a tremendous job of getting inside in the last few days of the attack. He and I wrote a story about it. There was also an excellent report by the Human Rights Watch team of Peter Bouckaert. At this point, with the UN mission having stopped, it looks as if this report will be the most definitive account of what went on in the camp.

Jenin, to me personally, is resonant because of my previous reporting in Afghanistan and limited reporting in Pakistan. People talk about the *Al-Jazeera* effect. But what's going on in Israel seems to resonate much more powerfully during this *intifada* than the last one. In part, this is due to satellite television. People are now seeing images immediately, and word is spreading much faster. I know from reporting in other Muslim countries, including Indonesia and Nigeria, that there is a tremendous resonance throughout the world. The perception is that the Western press and the Israelis are distorting things.

The Israeli Defence Forces (IDF) moved into the camp. And they correctly argued that the Jenin refugee camp was one of the largest centers for the suicide bombers coming out of the Occupied Territories. They had traced 23 suicide bombers to the camp. When we did get into it, we saw posters called martyr posters covering virtually every storefront, the walls of the local hospital, and the exterior walls of the youth center. These posters praise persons who have died in any kind of fighting or conflict with the Israelis. It could be a youth who has been shot at a checkpoint. It could be a gunman killed trying to invade a settlement. The suicide bombers receive their own martyr posters. One poster I saw represented a suicide bomber as a martyr, a hero, a giant, and then had his name. There are also many posters for Palestinian leaders who were assassinated by Israel, usually in helicopter or bombing attacks. So the martyr posters are not just glorifying suicide bombers. They're glorifying anyone who dies for the cause. The Palestinian Authority pays for the printing of the posters.

The actual attack started on April 3. Both sides misjudged what was about to happen. During a previous incursion, the Israeli army had come up to the edges of the camp but had not actually penetrated into it. Palestinians who decided to defend the camp this time—fighters who survived—told us they did not expect the Israelis to come in all the way. They didn't think the Israelis had the guts to go into the center of the camp.

The camp itself is very small. It's about a square kilometer packed with narrow alleyways—a very difficult area to enter and fight. It was also packed with civilians. About 13,000 or 14,000 people lived in this very small area. The fact that the Palestinians didn't expect the Israelis to come all the way into the camp, I think, led many Palestinian families and civilians to stay inside the camp. Some of them wanted to stay. They saw it as their duty to stay and resist the Israelis. They felt they had been refugees once. Many of the people in Jenin are originally from the city of Haifa. I also think there was peer pressure on families to stay in the houses. You'd be seen as a traitor if you were to leave.

The Israelis essentially expected very little resistance. During the previous incursion in March, most of the Palestinian fighters had fled out of the camp up onto a nearby hill. So the IDF actually sent in a reserve unit, not one of their regular army units, to take the camp.

The Israelis aren't giving exact numbers, but on the morning of April 3 as many as 1,500 to 2,000 Israeli soldiers started the attack. There were dozens of tanks and bulldozers and APCs involved. Inside the camp, there were only about 100-150 Palestinians armed with homemade bombs and Kalashnikov rifles. The incursion caused tremendous unity among the different Palestinian factions. The camp was a center for Hamas and Islamic Jihad, which are two of the more hard-line groups that back suicide bombing in Israel. Palestinian policemen joined them. In the past, the Palestinian police had tried—not very hard—to control Hamas and Islamic Jihad.

Now, the policemen who had once tried to arrest these extremists were fighting alongside them to defend the camp. And that's something you see throughout the Occupied Territories today—a tremendous sense of solidarity among Palestinians who were divided in the past. There is also tremendous support for Arafat in the wake of all this.

The Fiercest Fighting in Israeli History

When the attack started on April 3, the Israelis had a surprisingly difficult time entering the area. The lanes into the camp are so narrow that they were unable to get any of their armored vehicles through them. They decided to bring in bulldozers and start clearing lanes from all different directions to penetrate to the center of the camp. But even after three days, they were still not doing very well. Israeli officials during this attack told me they had run into astonishing resistance, the fiercest fighting they had ever found in Israeli history. This is a strong statement coming from the Israeli army. On April 6, three days into the attack, the Israelis started using Cobra helicopters to fire accurate wire-guided missiles into buildings where Palestinian fighters were holed up. They made more headway with that tactic.

Three days later, on April 9, came the pivotal moment in the fight for Jenin. The Israelis had made more progress. They had surrounded a neighborhood called Hawashin, which was located on the eastern part of the camp. Israeli officials told us that four reservists entered a small courtyard. Palestinians ambushed and killed them. Then nine Israeli soldiers tried to go in and retrieve their bodies, and they were also shot to death.

There were many press reports of a suicide bomber going in and killing the Israeli reservists. But it was actually a conventional ambush. According to the Palestinians in the camp, after the ambush, after six days of frustration and the loss of 13 soldiers—an enormous amount when you consider that the Israelis lost only one soldier in the attack on the nearby city of Nablus—the IDF intensified use of the helicopters. They increased the number of missiles fired.

They also brought in many more D-9 armored bulldozers. These American-made bulldozers are almost two stories tall, with an enormous shovel in front and a spike in the back used to rip into houses and knock them down. The driver sits in a big metal case. They're terrifying vehicles. The bulldozers were used much more indiscriminately after that ambush. Instead of simply clearing lanes, the bulldozers started knocking down whole swathes of houses. Two days later, on April 11, Palestinian resistance ended in the camp. Throughout the attack, one of the problems was that the ICRC and other humanitarian groups were barred from access to the camp. There were no ambulances allowed into the camp. The Israelis said that they did allow the ambulances to go in and that the Palestinian drivers were afraid of going in; but the Palestinian drivers said that, when they entered the camp, the Israelis fired on them. You constantly ended up with this sort of he-said, she-said contradiction.

Although the fighting essentially ended on April 11, the Israelis continued to block access to the camp for at least three more days. This was a big problem.

There were immediate claims from Palestinian officials in Ramallah—not the Palestinians in Jenin—that hundreds of Palestinian civilians had been killed in a massacre. The casualty totals according to the Human Rights Watch report are 52 Palestinians dead, 22 of them civilians. So there were roughly 30 Palestinian fighters and 23 Israeli soldiers killed. The Israelis argue that this shows there was no massacre and that they had taken great care during the attack on the camp. There was a single documented case of a wounded woman who might have survived if she had gotten medical care. She lived for 36 hours after being wounded before she bled to death. Her house was only 200 or 300 yards from a local hospital.

There were isolated cases of surrendering prisoners being shot. One case involved a guy who was a diabetic. Typically, Palestinian men were forced to take off their shirts because the Israelis feared they were wearing bombs. This diabetic man was carrying a bag of his clothes and his insulin, and apparently, when he moved too quickly, an Israeli soldier panicked and shot him. There are, I would say, a half-dozen cases of prisoners being shot, but there was no clear evidence of systematic executions.

Ironically, for the Palestinian fighters Jenin was a tremendous victory, because it represented an amazing kill ratio for them, almost 1:1. During the first *intifada*, I believe, the casualty rate was 5:1. During the second *intifada*, Hamas considered it a victory when the ratio was 3:1, three Palestinians killed for every Israeli.

There were three questionable Israeli practices. One that you don't hear much about, but which has been used for a long time by the Israeli army, is to declare a curfew in a town after it has been taken, allowing no one to go outside, and enforcing the ban with deadly force by firing at anyone who ventures out. There were at least three such victims killed in Jenin town, which is around the refugee camp. One of them was a 14-year-old boy. We saw this ourselves. The Israeli soldiers were very aggressive in using this tactic.

In the center of the camp, where the ambush of the Israeli soldiers occurred, the Israeli army bulldozed about 100 homes in apparent retribution for what had occurred there. The Israeli army insisted that the destruction had simply been caused by an effort to make lanes wide enough for tanks to come in. But when you actually stood in the center of the camp, it was like standing in the center of a football field, completely cleared.

The Use of Human Shields in House to House Searches

The most troubling tactic used throughout the Jenin attack, a tactic in other attacks as well, was the consistent use of Palestinians as human shields. Israeli soldiers would take a house. Then they would have a Palestinian man walk in front of them down the street so they could go to the next house. The Palestinian man would knock on the door. Then the Israeli soldiers would force the Palestinian to go through the different rooms in the house, and open drawers, for fear of booby-traps. We heard consistent accounts of this practice from different Palestinians.

That's it. Essentially, there was no massacre. But there were serious questions about the conduct of the IDF during what went on there.

I'm curious to hear your thoughts and your reactions to the lack of a UN mission in Jenin. It was hard for me to judge, when I was there, what the perceptions were on the outside. The ICRC was in a very difficult position. I interviewed officials about the lack of access and tried to get quotes from them complaining about not being allowed into the camp for eight or eleven days. Generally, they did not comment on it.

My last question would be whether there is a double standard here, because there wasn't much of an outcry that the weapons systems used by the Israelis—Cobra helicopters, M16s, and these bulldozers—were American. I'm also happy to talk about Afghanistan, where I did some reporting, and questions about the U.S. bombing there. I believe Human Rights Watch is doing a report now on the extent of the civilian casualties.

I would like to bring up another example of the issues that we talked about. I interviewed Israeli soldiers involved in the attack. They said they viewed themselves as victims. They said this was an issue of Israel's very existence. They believe that Palestinians are carrying out a genocidal campaign against Jews. Palestinians saw it the opposite way. Maybe that's a requirement of war. But it was very clear in this situation.

G.M. Tamás: It is quite difficult to reply to this. An academic is used to sustaining or refuting a thesis and coming up with a counter-thesis. And you have very carefully avoided presenting anything that would have made my job easier. So, instead, I shall reply with a story of my own.

What can one do? I went to Israel for the first time in my life last December, and I encountered some cousins I haven't seen in 30 years. They had emigrated from Romania. One of them is my age and her son is a soldier, drafted into the army. She's on the left. She helps to bring truckloads of food to the camps when she can, and she has demonstrated and contributed money to Arab causes.

At the same time, she is packing clothes and food for her son who, in the morning, is leaving for the front. Now, the question is, what does she say to him? Does she say, "You are fighting for the wrong cause. I am against what you're doing. But you're my son." Or does she just say, "Go, darling, and we'll see." That's what she says, actually. Or, should she convince him to desert?

You know there is an option in the Israeli army. You can say that you won't serve. I don't know how long this will be the case.

And he will say to his mother, "You are a diaspora Jewess. You don't understand. You are naturally on the side of minorities, of the underdog. But we have a country to defend."

Now, you said that the members of this generation of military-service age have to convince themselves that revenge is absolute, that the Palestinians want to exterminate them all. And the Palestinian youth have to do the same.

So, as a thesis—I'm trying to create one—let's say this is a situation in which moral and political decisions are very much dependent on knowledge. Is it indeed true that one of the parties, or both of them, wants to exterminate the other? Is it indeed the case that there is an absolute danger? Is it indeed the case that decency is not allowed? Because if you had sufficient grounds to accept that the country is in mortal danger, that all of its inhabitants will be exterminated in the case of a victory by the opponent, then, of course, brutal tactics can be excused. So is this true? Can this be known?

And this is where the media are important—as are people who have the power and ability to speak out in public. Not just professional journalists, but also human rights activists, politicians, and these famous people, who, for some reason, are asked to put forward a point of view.

Do we know? Can we judge really? Because I guess that our judgment on military tactics, brutality, and so on, must be dependent on what we know about the dangers involved. If we must protect ourselves against genocide or the other side must, then this demands, necessitates, and legitimizes different kinds of military tactics.

And in war, people are partisan. They are always prepared to say the other side is up to no good and might really kill off all civilians if it has the opportunity. So, my question would be, how far from reality are the perceptions of the Palestinians and of the Israelis—I mean the real bearers of majority opinion—about the dangers they are encountering? That's one question. You know the answer better than I do.

Also, to what extent is it true that these perceptions, rather than accounting for the conduct of the war, are creating military strategies and policies? If they are, what do you think we can do about it?

False Perceptions of a Genocidal Campaign

David Rohde: The thesis I should have presented was this: The Israeli right wing creates a false perception about the Palestinians and about what's going on there. I think there is a false perception of a genocidal campaign to wipe out Israelis. I think the majority of Palestinians accept Israel's existence. Other reporters have spent several hours with Sharon—I have not—and they say he sincerely believes Israel's existence is threatened. But his rhetoric—which frames every attack in terms of a genocidal campaign against Jews—creates tremendous problems of perception. It adds poison to an already extremely poisonous atmosphere. In the Israeli right wing, they talk of an Arab mentality. They say Arabs only respect strength. Therefore, Israel must respond with overwhelming force whenever there's a Palestinian attack.

What surprised me about the conflict was—to Israel's credit—how incredibly strong and vibrant the country is at this point. What it has achieved after 54 years is amazing. So the Palestinians don't need to be shown again how strong Israel is. This tactic doesn't seem to be working. It just seems to be creating even worse perceptions on the Palestinian side.

I sense that there was less of an outcry about the UN investigation, particularly in the United States, because Israel was the country in question. If it had been a different situation—let's say, with a UN team trying to go into Serbia—there would have been a much higher level of condemnation.

It was not a massacre of hundreds of people. But the international reaction was nevertheless different. If an African government had done what the Israeli government did in Jenin, you would not have had this reaction, this hesitation, or this extending of the benefit of the doubt.

Aryeh Neier: I want to comment on the sending in of the UN team. I don't have any inside information. But I assume that when Kofi Annan appointed the UN team, he thought he had firm U.S. backing for its establishment. Clearly, along the way, the United States made a calculation that it had other interests that were more important. I think the United States calculated that negotiating freedom for Arafat took precedence so it agreed with the Israelis not to back the effort to send in the UN team. The U.S. made a very tepid statement when the Israelis absolutely blocked the team from going in. In effect, it undercut the United Nations by doing so, because the UN had put its own credibility on the line by designating the team. If this trade-off was made, it is quite unfortunate. It undermines the possibility that the UN can credibly organize investigations in other circumstances. If the Israelis can simply stonewall an investigation with such a high profile, a higher profile than any UN investigation I can think of, then everybody will know that they do not have to go along with that kind of UN investigation in the future. The whole idea of these kinds of investigations was killed off by the way this took place.

David Rohde: I'd just add that the events in Jenin have played into the sense of victimization we were speaking about. I think we've seen this same phenomenon in Al Qaeda's training camps. During its indoctrination of recruits, Al Qaeda stresses the victimization of Muslims and points to a vast Judeo-Christian conspiracy to conquer and enslave or exterminate all Muslims. Jenin will be cited. Chechnya is constantly cited. So are Kashmir and Bosnia. In this sense the inaction in Srebrenica has come back to haunt us, because Al Qaeda cites it.

What's striking to me and other reporters is the spread of this sort of fundamentalist ideology. It is very popular, sophisticated, and appealing, especially to children of Muslim immigrants living in Europe and elsewhere. There are very educated children, for example, of Pakistani immigrants in Britain, who are completely turned off by Western materialism, by a sense of emptiness in Western culture, and, more than anything else, by racism. All of this waiting and not acting and not dealing with these problems by the United States, not taking responsibility for its own failures in terms of addressing grievances in the Muslim world, is coming back to haunt us. I think some of the grievances are exaggerated, obviously. But it's important now that we don't simply see ourselves as victims.

Both Sides Identify as Victims and Winners

Sonja Licht, Fund for an Open Society-Serbia board: Tamás was talking about the issue of truth. Who is going to find out the real truth about whether someone's group or nation is feeling that they are in mortal danger? We need to think seriously about how different organizations, different groups dealing with policy, can approach this issue of how to find out what is the real truth in such a situation. Not only to describe the situation, but to determine who is individually endangered by whom. Is there truth in it? If there is, if someone is in absolute danger, how can one struggle to make this truth known? At one point, we believe that the media are enough. Well, they are not. Many people don't trust the media. They are, at the same time and for many reasons, good and not so good. I think we are at a crossroads. We have to think seriously about how to go about answering Tamás's question.

I've spoken with a number of people who were directly involved in the negotiations between the Israelis and the Palestinians in recent months. They told me that one of the things that made them very concerned is that both sides not only feel that they are the victims, but also believe themselves to be the winners. We know this situation quite well in my own region. Sometimes it's very difficult to decide which is the prevalent feeling. Of course, those who are being killed are first and foremost victims. But those who are leading them are sometimes quite convinced that, by having these victims, they are the winners. I don't know what Mr. Arafat or Mr. Sharon were thinking, or whether they believe in what they are doing. But I definitely know that the last suicide bomb, just two days ago, proved to all of us trying seriously to understand the situation, that there are people on both sides who do not want the situation to be sorted out in a genuine, serious way.

I think we simply have to deal with this problem in a much more serious way than we have until now. I don't know who must deal with it or how. I don't think the human rights groups are enough. They can do one kind of reporting. But I believe that the international community, which is probably best still represented by the UN, should be much more serious in trying to approach the question of the truth, as much as it is possible in this very complex and difficult conflict.

G.M. Tamás: I'd just like to add something I have experienced directly. I had a fantastic opportunity, because my publisher in Paris—it is a small publishing house—happens to be Arab. I asked him to introduce me to people from the Algerian Armed Islamic Group (GIA). This was a few years ago. The young people tried to explain to me what they were about. And you know, this is one of the bloodiest movements anywhere. They are not killing foreigners in Algeria anymore, because there aren't any foreigners left in Algeria. Now they are killing their compatriots, seemingly at random sometimes, in order to gain support and to intimidate the state structures.

I asked these two young people whether it is a fact that they are fundamentalist religious extremists. And they told me something very familiar. They said, "Oh God, no. Who would believe in all this crap? Who reads the Koran anyway? We read in

French mostly." And so there was this contempt, this absolute refusal to deal in a straightforward manner. This is part of what we know in this part of the world, where very sophisticated, well-educated, well-read people—for example, among right-wing populaces—will turn to the public and pretend they are simplistic and traditionalistic while we know perfectly well they're not.

We all know these people. They cast the political language of discontent and resistance in terms that they suppose people would like to hear. Posturing and pretense and the treatment of tradition in simplistic, insincere ways is a game we play in Eastern Europe. We understand perfectly well that when politicians in Eastern Europe tell an audience that we are like medieval king number five, both the politician and the audience and the commentators know that this is complete nonsense. Nobody means it. But the consequences are there. These days in Hungary we have plenty of opportunities to observe this phenomenon. This is a game in these countries with wounded identities. So it is very difficult to find out what people really mean.

I am not an expert on Israel, but, as a sympathetic, concerned, and worried observer, I can see that the use of political language is the same as in Eastern Europe. After all, Israelis got to Israel from Eastern Europe. They are not so far from our political culture. According to political science professor Shlomo Avineri, Poland is the key to understanding Israel. And so it is. Of course, Israelis will always refer to the Holocaust and to the millennia of anti-Semitism and to genocidal practices and thoughts. Some mean it. Some don't. Some half mean it. Some don't. Arabs too harbor genuine complaints. And, of course, it is very difficult to find out what people really want. If you walk around in Tel Aviv, you might think that people only want freedom and welfare and good wine. But the Israeli politicians won't tell you this, because it does not fit into the prevailing national myth. It seems perverse.

So, while this kind of discourse is dominant, it is impossible for journalists from New York not to treat all of it as another fact of war. This is sometimes what we feel. I and other ruthless liberals in Eastern Europe might sometimes consider the speech of our opponents dishonest and deceptive, though they are, you know, our own compatriots. So, it is very complicated. World opinion and people who are indeed trying to deal with all this are always in a hurry and have to consider the hard facts, and the hard facts are, of course, corpses and bullets and buildings and so on. It is extremely difficult. I think the solution should be really political. And if the Israelis and the Palestinians cannot convince themselves to talk honestly about water and territory and fears, I don't know what we can do.

I do agree with the human rights groups. They can count the number of corpses and humiliations, and document murderous talk. But what can you do from outside? This is why, for example, I don't share the dominant myth in Eastern Europe that our joining the European Union will solve everything. If we don't solve our own problems, nobody will do it for us. This is why I'm pessimistic. The two sides don't show any signs of becoming more rational. And our rationalism from outside seems pretentious and unfeeling.

Videotapes, Headlines, and the Search for Truth

David Rohde: The leadership is not rational. And average people on both sides see some kind of two-state solution as a way to end this.

On the broader theme of a truth, or the truth, today there is more information out there in the world than ever before. But it doesn't seem to matter. People will dismiss anything, be it videotapes, photographs, statements, so long as it doesn't fit their ideology. I feel that my work is futile sometimes. It is a frustrating but very important phenomenon that people dismiss these things. I don't know why it's happening. But I see it in all the different countries I visit.

We have to keep trying and digging. There is a truth, I think, to what happened in Jenin. I think the Human Rights Watch report essentially captured it.

Samantha Power: I have a question for David about working for the *New York Times*. I was struck by a headline that accompanied a news story on the publication of the Human Rights Watch report. The headline was, I believe: "Human Rights Report Finds Massacre Did Not Occur in Jenin." The second paragraph said, "Oh, but lots of war crimes did." Why wouldn't they make the war crimes the headline and the non-massacre the second paragraph?

I have Jewish friends who think that whenever a Palestinian boy or child is killed it inevitably ends up on the front page of the *New York Times*, whereas suicide-bomber photos are always inside the paper. I mean, it agrees with your point. People read publications as they choose to read them. But can you give some sense, without speaking out of school, about how politicized it feels to be reporting from Israel compared to all the other places that you've reported from. How are these decisions made vis-à-vis photos, headlines, placement? And where do the pressures come from?

David Rohde: I think there is more pressure writing about Israel than any other place in the world. At the *New York Times* you feel as if you're being watched like a hawk. And it makes you much more careful about the allegations you make. You're accused by both sides. Right now there's a boycott of the *New York Times* by Jewish groups in the United States that said our coverage has shifted from being anti-Israeli to anti-Semitic. And then, of course, the paper has a long-running reputation in the Arab world for being part of the Jewish-owned global conspiracy. And you're just more careful because editors are nervous about trying to get it right and trying to be fair. I was unhappy with some of the editing on that story and the way the wording was changed suddenly, I thought, to play down the war crimes.

I've had conversations with editors. Once, for example, the Israelis presented documents they said linked Arafat to terror. The proof wasn't quite there, however. The significance of the documents was an exaggeration by the Israeli side. One editor removed some nuance from the story, and the headline was "Documents Allege Arafat Terror Link." The documents don't allege that. I think it's a bias. And there are biases. Israel is an extremely emotional issue to American Jews. This doesn't mean that they carry it over into their work, but it's a reality there. I was really proud of the reporting we did on Jenin. I think we were very fair in what we did. But no one believes it. So what does it matter?

András Mink, Open Society Archives, program coordinator, Hungarian Services: I have a speculative question for Professor Tamás. You said that knowledge plays an important role in assessing the morality and justifiability of certain military actions. We can easily imagine a situation in which sufficient knowledge is not available at the moment when we decide to use certain means. This was partly the case of the Second World War. Sometimes we can get knowledge of the true nature and real threat of our enemies only after the enemy has been defeated. On the other hand, to defeat the enemy, we used very brutal means that could be justified only after the fact.

G.M. Tamás: I won't go into the philosophy of it, but this is one of the most important questions. What I meant was much more modest basically. It was just a very sentimental and commonplace warning that we should try, without too much skepticism, to access what is really the truth about the motivations and the actions and the intentions of parties. This will always be dependent on the frameworks of our understanding.

How do you start a revolution, for example? Starting a revolution—insofar as it is started consciously by anybody, but sometimes it happens—depends on the opinion you make of the society you try to overturn and to change, which sometimes is called knowledge. It's based upon judgments taken from economics and sociology and history and so on. So is war.

For example, is it indeed the case that the whole Israeli political establishment is determined not to tolerate a Palestinian state? I mean a real Palestinian state. And is Israel a danger to a lasting Middle East peace or not? This is dependent on detailed historical and political knowledge. Mr. Rohde has said that he knows that a part of these people are indeed committed to a two-state solution. How strong are they politically? Of course, things change. So, it's not impossible.

I didn't mean anything very profound really. But we know that the critical and self-critical sides in a conflict are usually not known to the opposition. Think of the Yugoslav conflict. How many Serbs knew, during the worst days of the conflict, that not all Croats wanted to eat all Serbs alive? Very few, although it was indeed perfectly documented in the same language. And, you know, I have just read an article in *Le Monde Diplomatique*, which is a very reasonable, very intelligent assessment of the Israeli-Arab conflict. And, of course, it won't be published in the mass press in Cairo.

The question is more than epistemological. Are we prepared to influence all the parties concerned, to be aware of all this? Let me just expand upon what you were talking about with regard to the *New York Times*. What is reported about the Israeli-Arab conflict in the Hungarian press? We have four national dailies, three of them left liberal, one right wing. The three left-liberal dailies won't publish a single critical word about Israel. There is one commentator who sometimes will criticize Israel in very measly terms. A headline that reads "No Genocide but War Crimes in Jenin" would be out of the question. It would be considered a nasty thing, because, indeed, we face active anti-Semitic movements here. And the sensitivity of journalists is about 200 times larger than in New York and New Jersey. On the other hand, the right-wing national daily won't publish a single word favorable to Israel. Therefore, people, including myself, won't try to get information from the Hungarian press regarding the Middle East conflict. This has nothing to do with Israel or the Arabs. It has to do with the situation of the Jewish minority in Hungary.

You know, nobody is interested in the least about what the facts really are. I should have said, "Okay, let's try to get interested in the facts." I didn't say anything deeper than that.

The Rational Motives of Suicide Bombers

David Rohde: I think the facts are out there. And what is going on involves a rational process. Take the suicide bombers. They are usually taking revenge for specific assassinations or killings of Palestinian leaders. A colleague of mine interviewed a guy who was a suicide bomber. When he got to his target—a big crowd of Israelis—he pushed the button but nothing happened, and he was arrested. He and a couple friends had been involved in radical Palestinian movements. One of their friends was killed, and they decided to carry out an operation. The word goes out that someone wants to carry out an operation, someone who is angry, say someone who has lost a relative. The young man who carried out the horrible bombing at the Passover gathering had apparently tried to go to Jordan six months earlier to marry his fiancé. The Israeli forces wouldn't let him cross into Jordan. He was completely enraged by this and then disappeared. His family didn't know where he was. Then he ended up carrying out the bombing. So, it's not as blind as it appears.

I would not read all the stories about Israel before I went there, because it just seemed so depressing and illogical. I don't know how we get past that. But I am somewhat optimistic again because of the general sense I get, listening to both sides, that average people are more reasonable than the rhetoric you hear.

Joost Hiltermann: Just a brief comment on the use of language, and the use of Islam, and saying that all these attacks are inspired by Islam, that they are part of the religion. You hear this a lot. I lived for many years on the West Bank. The people who are deeply religious are usually not the people who carry out these attacks. The attackers are younger people who are alienated in many ways or angered in many ways and then recruited by movements that use religion in a political way. They do all kinds of things that are absolutely not religious at all. Killing and targeting civilians are prohibited in Islam. What drives most people is not some vision of an Islamic state, which is completely made up. For most people, what matters is what happens when they get up in the morning, when they go to work, during the day, and when they go home. And what happens is that there is a soldier standing right on top of him. There is constant humiliation. There are petty restrictions that Palestinians face during the military occupation that drive them up the wall. In a way they don't even care anymore about people being killed among themselves. They care about not being able to carry out their daily lives. And so they will gather around any ideology that promises to bring a savior. They will name their children after the latest hero, whether he be Saddam Hussein or George Bush. Children are named after whoever happens to be promising, at that very moment, to deliver the Palestinians from their misery. The ideology is completely based upon this.

At heart, people just want the occupation to end and to have some kind of state. People are nationalists, if anything, if you want an ideology. It's not because they believe in nationalism as an ideology but mostly because they don't want the situation that they are in.

Fred Abrahams: I have a question for David that builds upon Joost's point. It is about the camp in Jenin. Who administered the camp? How could it have been tolerated if such difficult living conditions existed there? Unfortunately, it is in many ways predictable or understandable that when refugees are crammed into such close and constrained quarters there would be a growing resentment, hatred, anger, frustration, and so on. Just building on my experience with the KLA in Kosovo, while there were clearly some people with nationalist aims, the vast majority of villagers were in exactly the same kind of situation Joost described. They were having to deal with getting stopped and humiliated by the police on the way to the market or not being able to study in their language or not being able to go to the hospital and be treated fairly. So was the camp a simmering cauldron of discontent? Why was that tolerated?

David Rohde: It was a cauldron. But what fuels the discontent has less to do with poverty, I think, than with the Israeli presence around the camp. It has to do with power. It's just like an arrogant cop, whether he's Hungarian or American or whatever, who bullies you. You resent it tremendously. When it's a foreigner, it's that much stronger. The UN ran the camp. There were bomb factories inside the UN-run camp. This explains the rational Israeli distrust of the UN and the UN fact-finding mission. It's not crazy. They're not killing each other because of pure hate. It's fear. That's what is really driving it. On the Israeli side, they don't have checkpoints, but they're afraid all the time. You walk down the streets and look carefully at every person carrying a backpack. You're always on edge. And the Palestinians know it's an effective tactic, because every single Israeli is always wondering about the person standing near them. So, it's fear on both sides. They feed each other.

I agree that there is no military solution to this conflict. Israel just arrested many of the top Palestinian militants. But there will be more to replace them in a few months. I think a large fence is the way to go: Some kind of settlement, which most Israelis support, with a fence, and abandonment of most of the settlements. This is possible. They were very close in Camp David. It sounds strange now, but I do think a solution is within reach. It's just a question of getting the two sides to sit down and do it and stop the cycle of recrimination.

III.

Personal vs. Government Accountability

Moderator: *Aryeh Neier*
Speaker: *Samantha Power*
Comments: *Shalini Randeria*, Max Weber Professor of Sociology,
University of Munich

Samantha Power: I will talk about accountability in two ways. First, very briefly, I'll talk about the people who commit crimes and the relationship between them and accountability and responsibility. And second, the aspect I know more about, the problem of bystander accountability. In terms of the perpetration of crimes, the thing that is lost in ethnic conflict, as we all know, is a conception of personal identity and responsibility. Whole groups become accountable for the real or perceived crimes of a few. Perpetrators of crimes and demonizers of other ethnic groups become the guardians. They see themselves as the guardians of their whole collectives, and they see themselves as victims, of course. While they possess multiple identities–as teachers, husbands, fathers, Muslims, Serbs, Tutsis–their sense of identity becomes narrowed and one form of identity–ethnic, national, or religious–comes to drown out all the others.

There are a couple of structural problems when it comes to a government's role in dealing with these crimes. One is that ethnically targeted violence is usually committed by governments–that is, states that are all too successful, states that are too intrusive in people's lives, states that are tyrannies. The Rwanda case and the Nazi case are obvious examples. These involved groups or entities that manufactured fear and invoked–and usually manipulated–historical experience in the service of some relatively well-defined cause. So, that's one form of the governmental role. The other is, of course, the failed state, or failing state, where more noxious elements have the opportunity to thrive and where a government either won't or can't contain the violence.

Given the state role, or state-contrived or state-related nonrole, government accountability for these crimes is quite difficult to achieve. We've talked about ways in which it can be achieved over time, whether through international accountability, or through regime change. I think the healthiest way, or the most viable, long-term way, for societies to deal with crimes committed in their name is for there to be some kind of regime change and for accountability to become one mechanism, among many, to achieve a political end. In such a situation, you're using somebody's relationship to past abuses to score political points. This seems to be the Nazi case. The younger generation rebelled against the earlier generation, and dealing with the crimes committed became part of a local historical, political, and cultural process.

The international community can play the role of an outside guardian of a set of principles. International tribunals and other mechanisms can play a role in supplying a historical record and removing the legitimacy of certain individuals and certain ways of behaving. But it seems the best role for tribunals is to serve as a vehicle for a local domestic process. Since it is unlikely that governments will play such a role on their own, it is up to successor governments or movements, or nongovernmental bottom-up pressure. But these pressures are hard to muster in failed states or tyrannical states.

The aspect of this I know most about involves not the people who commit the crimes, but the people who allow them to be committed. This touches on the psychology and the structural impediments to taking responsibility and suppressing war crimes, crimes against humanity, genocide. I will talk now about the assuming of personal and governmental accountability for America's bystanding.

Genocide and the U.S. Response of Silence

First of all, let me summarize my findings after seven years of looking at America's responses to genocide in the 20th century. I've examined the Armenia case, the Holocaust, the effort to ratify the genocide convention—an effort that took more than forty years and yielded a very self-protective, imperfect result, but a ratification nonetheless—Cambodia, the case of Iraq killing nearly 100,000 rural Kurds in 1988, the Bosnia case, and Rwanda. I worked with the National Security Archive, a Washington nongovernmental group, that gets the U.S. government to declassify documents in order to excavate the internal rationalizations and rationales for particular policy decisions. I interviewed about 300 U.S. officials and people who either influenced U.S. policy or were in close proximity to those who did.

Basically, what one finds across the century is not just a policy of nonintervention, in the sense of nonmilitary intervention. The policy is one of noninvolvement. (Bosnia, actually, was the exception.) Genocide, especially, is greeted again and again with a policy of silence and absolute structural shutdown. It almost seems as though the more extreme the abuses, the less the response mustered by the United

States. You get very little denunciation, and no use of the word genocide to describe a crime underway. No American president or senior official has ever used the word genocide to describe an ongoing crime, though they use it retrospectively from time to time. There is a reluctance to freeze the foreign-held assets of perpetrators, to impose any form of economic sanctions, to threaten prosecution in any kind of proactive way. Arms embargoes don't get imposed. Arms embargoes don't get lifted. Safe areas are not made safe. The United States plays very little role rallying troops from other countries if it is not willing to muster its own or to use its airlift and logistics capabilities to support peacekeepers or others who are prepared to confront atrocities. There is an all-systems shutdown.

In the 1990s, there was a successful campaign to establish a form of accountability. Claims by David Scheffer, the State Department's ambassador on war crimes during the Clinton administration, notwithstanding, this campaign was very much a political salve, at least in its original conception. Then it was taken up by people who were sincerely committed to international justice.

The second thing you see again and again is that, in the United States, genocide and crimes of this nature are greeted with society-wide silence. There isn't very much bottom-up pressure. There is also very little bureaucratic dissent within the U.S. government. Regarding Bosnia, under Bush Sr., you had low-level officials contesting the stances of their higher-ups. Under Clinton, you had the Cabinet split right down the middle, into two camps within the government. This dissent was legitimated by heavy press coverage and strong editorial support for involvement. As a result of this bureaucratic dissent, there was a strong, meaningful congressional role. With this kind of society-wide noise, you got denunciation, economic sanctions, and eventually, for political reasons, military intervention.

But in none of the other genocides do you see anything resembling this response. When you contrast the way the United States responded to the genocide in Bosnia—a much more robust response than to any other genocide in the 20th century—you get none of those pressures, none of those cleavages within government.

This was a summary of the findings. Now to the larger question, the issue of personal and governmental accountability for standing by.

American Alibis for Inaction on Genocide

There is practically no one assuming personal responsibility. You just don't find it. It is extraordinary. We spoke earlier about "not being there" being its own alibi. The man in my study who did the most to stop genocide, perhaps, was General Romeo

Dallaire, the Canadian commander in Rwanda. And he feels the worst about it. He's accepted more personal responsibility than any other individual I've been able to find, because he was there and because every day he was making decisions about whom to save and whom to walk away from. He lives with these decisions. And he has accepted full personal responsibility—to an exaggerated and unfortunate extent, I think.

This is in contrast to American officials who remained securely removed from the scene of the crime and who indeed pulled out the peacekeepers from under Dallaire. There is no formal mechanism, no congressional mandate, to look back formally and summon U.S. officials to answer questions like: "Where were you? Why did you do what you did? Why not radio jamming? Why not denunciation? Why not U.S. troops?" None of these questions were asked of U.S. officials. I was shocked, again, to encounter so many of them in my reporting who would turn to me and say, "Well, what's the answer? Why didn't we? What did he say? What did she say?" They have no idea. They, themselves, never compared notes. It was more convenient to move forward and not look back.

The hands-on relationship with the crisis was also so diffuse. There was no formal mechanism, no incentive in journalism, and no capacity to do any kind of excavation into the decision-making process after the fact. The reality is that people move on to the next problem, to the next crisis, to the next documentation of a massacre. Yesterday was yesterday.

The idea of looking back, reexamining situations in which decisions were taken to not get involved, is not something editors are going to deploy their journalists to do. We're bad enough at documenting sins of commission. But investigating sins of omission attracts less attention. I wouldn't have been able to take the time to do the job right, to establish personal responsibility, and to name names rather than merely present a broad, faceless picture, if it hadn't been for the support of the Open Society Institute. This work takes time. It is really hard to get people to talk to you. You have to get the goods before they will have the incentive to open up to you. It's a very laborious and resource-intensive task. So, to sum up, there is no formal responsibility, no personal accountability.

Thirdly, in terms of personal responsibility, individuals have a series of alibis that are available to them when they've been involved in taking decisions not to become involved, or taking decisions not to take a decision. One alibi, one you hear a lot by perpetrators of the crimes themselves, is that of the "cog in the bureaucracy." The alibi is based on a sense of no empowerment. "Well, I wanted to do X. But what could I really have done? How could I move the aircraft carrier?" You feel so small in these big governments. This is especially true, as is always the case, when there is no executive leadership in support of acting robustly in response to atrocities. Usually, there is executive leadership against acting at all. So the sense of "Who am I to do this or that?" or "How can I do this or that?" really allows people to walk away after the fact without looking inward.

Another alibi is something that James Thompson, during the Vietnam War, called the "ethicacy trap." Those who do care feel as if it is their job not to leave or to protest, but to work within the system, to play the game. In Rwanda and Cambodia, you had individuals who really cared about the atrocities being committed. But they censored themselves. They didn't believe their higher-ups wanted to hear about it. They believed there wasn't much that could be done, given that U.S. troops had been taken off the table. They told themselves that it would be better to plod along, better to work within, and say later, "Oh well, there was that one individual whose plight I was able to publicize, and who I was able to save." These people are consoled by the feeling that they were more effective working quietly within the system than they would have been loudly and noisily dissenting in any sort of serious or subversive way.

A third alibi involves a low-level, high-level distinction. On the low level, people say, "Look, I pushed the information up the chain. I'm not a person who's going to decide. I mean, how am I...?" It's back to the "cog in the bureaucratic machine." But this is a little different. It is "I did my part. It's not that I can't change the system. But I did my part to change what was coming out of government." These people again tend to self-censor. They give up after finding out that nothing has been done up top the first time. You ask for this. You report that. Nothing happens. Then why bother?

A fourth alibi involves high-level officials. They need to find more convincing alibis, because they're the ones who are further removed from the scene of the crime. They're not desk officers. They've never met Rwandans. They're dealing with a whole series of crises every day. So their alibis are more seductive and more important. The main one is context. Context is everything. As they go forward in their lives, they tell themselves a story about congressional opposition to involvement. People in the executive branch are quick to blame the Congress or the "American people" even if they have never attempted to engage them on the issue. Having a division of labor in the government gives everyone in each branch an alibi. You see this with the Rwanda experience. The administration people say, "It was the fault of the Congress. Go see the Congress." They defer to alleged public apathy or indifference or opposition to involvement. Again and again, you also see a deference to allied opposition. So, in the Bosnia case, people said, "The Europeans will never go along." And in the Rwanda case, they brought up Belgium and France and said, "If they're not doing it, why should we? We're taking our lead from people who actually know what they are doing in these regions."

Strategic Interests Rate a Higher Priority

And another alibi based upon context involves plain, old-fashioned strategic inter-est. It goes like this: "You know, we have an interest in being aligned with Saddam Hussein, even if he's gassing the Kurds." Strategic interest trumps until the presi-dent or the public makes genocide a priority. As long as other interests take priority, high officials do not try to convince the president to set a new agenda.

Finally, the other alibi related to high officials is knowledge. They can claim, be-cause there is usually a disconnect between the low level and the high level, not that they didn't know, but that they "didn't appreciate" the gravity of the situation on the ground. It's impossible to say you didn't know for two reasons. First, more than 50 years after the Holocaust, it sounds ridiculous; and second, the information is available to you in open sources. So you hear Clinton say in his Rwanda apology, "It may surprise you, but day after day, there were people like me sitting in offices who didn't fully appreciate the depth and the speed of the unimaginable horror which engulfed you." And the words "didn't fully appreciate" sound a lot like "I didn't have sexual relations with that woman" or "I didn't inhale." They are very Clintonian. But there is bureaucratic thinking at work here as well. Decision-makers decide what their priorities are up front; then others act upon them and decide what they feel the president appreciates. And they will bring what he appreciates to his attention.

Then there is the alibi that points to the futility of the proposed interventionary measures. It is the excuse that the options don't offer a solution. If you look at policy as a tool kit, they're saying things like: "This tool"—radio jamming, let's say—"what will it achieve?" "Economic sanctions, so what?" "Surely the only way to stop geno-cide is to confront the perpetrators militarily. Oh, but we don't want to do that." "But we can't do any of these other things either."

You can look back and tell a story about why we did what we did vis-à-vis Cambodia, the Holocaust, Armenia, and Rwanda, and you'll always find that there is a geopolitical context that will explain, if not excuse, the policy response, or lack of response. And this is where people are most prone to take shelter. It is only by putting the cases together that you realize there is a pattern of looking for and finding a geopolitical context to conceal the absence of will to stop genocide or atrocities.

Institutions have made efforts to establish accountability. There was the UN Srebrenica report and the Organization for African Unity (OAU) report on Rwanda. But there is a tendency in these reports, when the major powers or member states are invoked, to treat them as black-box entities, like "France," or "Belgium," or "the Clinton administration." This is a problem for several reasons. First, such a broad-brush indictment will not alter the behavior of the individual actors within governments. Governmental accountability is problematic in and of itself because people within governments don't necessarily identify with their governments. You can feel like a dissenter. You can invoke one of the alibis I just mentioned. And even if the government is blamed, you're not named.

Another problem is that without breaking down why the government has behaved in a certain way—and again this is true with committing crimes as well as allowing them to be committed—you're not actually learning anything. You're just demonizing an entity. Then you say, "Oh well, they sucked. And I, of course, would be different." We can always be forward-looking. "They didn't do the right thing, but I would behave differently, of course." And by judging and not understanding, you greatly minimize your capacity to identify with someone who does something or doesn't do something that has such immoral consequences. So broad-brush aspersions grounded in woeful policies are problematic. They are just like the phrase "Never again." "Never again" will the Clinton administration allow 800,000 Tutsis to be murdered between April and July of 1994. This is what such sweeping critiques amount to.

I would like to touch on one final issue involving accountability. It involves an incentive structure that is skewed against taking a stand, against summoning your higher-ups to do more in the face of atrocity. There is no gain. If you take such a stand as a bureaucratic actor, you run the risk of not being invited to the next meeting. You might be marginalized institutionally as emotional, soft, unrealistic. If you allow genocide to go forward, there is no cost at all. There is no danger that your name will be named; you're just part of the faceless mass of bureaucracy. Author Philip Gourevitch makes this point often, and I will steal it: You will get promoted. If you're Kofi Annan, you become the secretary-general. If you're Madeleine Albright, you become the secretary of state. But if you're General Dallaire, you become suicidal, broken by the stand that you have taken.

And there is also a disconnect with journalists. We, and I think David would agree with this, feel as if we have profited enormously professionally by taking the stands that we have taken on atrocities. I mean we don't report for this reason, I hope. But there is a disconnect between the treatment of journalists or people in civil society who take stands and that of persons in government who do so. The fortunes of these communities are very different.

It's incredibly important—as we think about accountability, especially when talking about standing by and watching—to name names and try, somehow, to get this issue into the cost-benefit calculus that politicians make reflexively day to day. It is important to increase the cost of doing nothing by at least creating some risk to reputation. I hope my book and other efforts have contributed. In doing so, you also legitimize those persons who dared to stand up, who are perhaps unemployed, or working as middle-school teachers, or starting human rights organizations, and perhaps feeling pretty washed up. I think it's really important for us to tell both stories as we think about how you can galvanize people to take up this kind of work especially if the Congress isn't going to do it and if there aren't formal mechanisms to examine governmental accountability and personal accountability for governmental policies.

How can we, from the outside, play a role affecting something that is, ultimately, reflexive but alterable in the minds of the policymakers? I think the proof that it is alterable is the footstep effect of even an insufficient form of accountability, the effect we saw in the late 1990s vis-à-vis Kosovo. Clinton administration officials feared that they would be held accountable, that it would be a third genocide "on their watch," and that they would have to live with the reputational stain of it for a very long time.

Destruction of Lives and Livelihoods at Gujarat, Western India

Shalini Randeria: I would like to share with you some experiences of the systematic pogrom against Muslims in Gujarat, a pogrom about which, surprisingly, there has been international silence. Since the first few days of violence in March 2002, there has not been much news about it in the European press.

I have just returned from Gujarat after having spent three weeks there, and my reasons for talking about the Gujarat experience are twofold. First, I think it is probably my best way of addressing some of the issues Samantha has raised, issues of both individual responsibility and governmental accountability. Muslims all over Gujarat have been targeted because the entire community is being collectively held responsible for the reprehensible acts of several hundred Muslims at Godhra. These Muslims burnt alive 58 Hindu right-wing religious activists and their family members by setting fire to the two railway compartments in which they were travelling on their way from Ayodhya, the site of the highly controversial Ram temple to be built in place of a medieval mosque. This gruesome incident on the 27th of February sparked off the month-long pogrom against Muslims.

More generally, of course, as Samantha has pointed out, ethnic violence is based not only on real or imagined recent grievances against entire groups but on a manipulation of historical memory and record as well. For many decades now Hindu right-wing propaganda has sought to mobilize hatred against all Indian Muslims by demonizing them as inherently cruel and intolerant and holding them responsible for centuries of real and imagined injustices and violence against Hindus during Mughal rule in precolonial India. Hindu perpetrators of crimes against Muslims in

Gujarat felt that they were not only avenging the deaths of fellow Hindus in Godhra but also righting the wrongs of history. As the supposed victims of history and defenders of their own community's honor, Hindus who are perpetrators or those who are complicit in aiding or abetting them—either in their official capacity as state bureaucrats or by turning a blind eye to the horrendous violence in their own neighborhoods—are all devoid of any feelings of guilt for the violence they have committed or which has been committed in their name. I was as shocked by the scale of the murder and rape of Muslim men and women and the destruction of their homes and property as I was by the widespread middle-class consensus in Gujarat that the Muslims deserved to be "taught a lesson" for the crimes committed by "them" in the past and the recent present.

Second, I'm a professional anthropologist and sociologist, but I also have an activist background as I come from the human rights movement in India. I was intimately involved with the first two human rights groups set up in Bombay and Delhi in the 1970s—so this is not the first time that I have seen civil rights violations. But the violence against the Muslims in Gujarat is not only on a scale never seen before in urban India but also qualitatively different in its extreme brutality, in its specific targeting of women and children, its widespread and planned destruction of Muslim homes, shops, and all means of livelihood and its state-sponsored and state-organized character. There has never been anything like it in post-independence India and I think it signals a rupture in the moral fabric of society and a breakdown of the secular multireligious state on the subcontinent, both of which will have serious consequences for Indian democracy in the future.

In responding to Samantha's presentation, I would like to make three points. First, I was struck by the fact that what I have recently witnessed in Gujarat is the very opposite of what she has described as the ideal case, in which mechanisms for establishing accountability take root and become part of a local democratic process. India is one of the world's largest democracies and by no means a failing or even a weak state. The state is capable of protecting the rights of its citizens, but it has chosen to do so only highly selectively. It is a democratic state with one of the worst records of human rights violations. The state has not only been directly responsible for such violations but has been complicit both in allowing such violations against specific ethnic or religious groups to occur and in not prosecuting the perpetrators—the police officers, army officers, local politicians or members of powerful communities and dominant castes. The violence against the Sikhs in the Indian capital following the murder of Prime Minister Indira Gandhi by her Sikh bodyguards showed this pattern.

In the case of Gujarat what is shamefully evident is not just the failure of the state to protect its most vulnerable citizens but its active complicity in these horrific crimes against the Muslims. The party in power, the BJP, has several organizations aligned to it which have systematically mobilized Hindus against Muslims and organized this spate of arson, looting, and rapes. The police, instead of doing something to stop the mobs and arresting those looting and burning shops and businesses belonging to Muslims in most of the major towns of Gujarat, actually incited the vandalizers—all middle-class men and women, not the poor or slum dwellers —"Go, go get your share of the Nike shoes. You're never going to get such a chance again."

Second, press reports have often condemned the breakdown of law and order, but in my opinion there has been no breakdown. Rather, the entire law and order machinery has been subverted and hijacked by the organizations affiliated with the Hindu right-wing party in power. Until the army moved in to restore order, the regional government, through its inaction, sent a signal that assured the perpetrators that they were free to loot, kill, burn, and rape Muslims as they pleased without fear of judicial consequences. The state absolved itself of any responsibility for the violence by insisting that the fury of the enraged majority was legitimate in the wake of the Godhra train burning. And they claimed that the government machinery, taken by surprise, was powerless to deal with such a large-scale "spontaneous" revenge by the masses. The few police officers who tried to restore order during the first few days of violence were punished by the Gujarat government through punitive transfers from their posts. This is in a sense the very opposite of the "ethicacy trap" that Samantha has described. The Gujarat trap catches those who not only decide to stay, but those who decide to do their duty and who do it successfully. The result is that they lose their jobs—not in the sense that they're out of work; but they are completely sidelined in their careers. And the signal sent to the bureaucracy is clear: they should serve the whims of their political masters even to the point of dereliction of duty and illegality.

Third, the looting and arson would have continued much longer had it not been for the pressure exercised by the national press and especially the television networks in Delhi. The private Star TV sent reporters to Gujarat who showed the looting and the burning of the shops on television, every day, 24 hours a day, as well as the inaction of the police in the face of this massive violence and destruction. As a result on the fourth day, the federal government, a coalition led by the same BJP, finally sent army troops to Gujarat. It was only then that the destruction of Muslim homes, shops and businesses could be stopped, though it took almost a month for some normalcy to be restored. By this time almost 2,000 Muslims had been killed.

And yet one can say that compared to other riots in urban India over the last 50 years this was not an unusually heavy loss of life. So that I think it would be correct to say that it was not a systematic genocide in Gujarat. It was a systematic, well-planned, and coordinated attempt to destroy the livelihoods of Muslims of all classes and occupations in towns and villages. In many parts of the state today there is not a single shop, a single hotel, a single restaurant or any business establishment belonging to a Muslim which is intact. Until now, in most riots the pattern of violence had always been either to stab or to kill, man-to-man. This is the first time women have been targeted, raped, and burnt alive in their homes. For the first time children have been snatched from the arms of their mothers or fathers and killed in front of them.

Government Abdication of Responsibility for Refugees

The rioters targeted Muslim property, including all household goods and even bicycles or bullock carts or agricultural implements, in order to destroy all means of livelihood. The Hindu nationalist plan seems to be to force Muslims to leave their homes and make it impossible for them to return. After every riot against Muslims in Gujarat, we have seen a migration of Muslims from mixed neighborhoods to Muslim residential areas. This kind of further ghettoization of the increasingly insecure Muslim communities makes them an easier target for the next round of sectarian violence.

There are at present some 100,000 Muslims in refugee camps in Gujarat, most of which receive only meager state funds. A government minister interviewed on television said, "Oh, don't you see? There is no need for state support. The Muslim community is taking care of its own camps. So you see civil society is functioning well." It is a travesty of the idea of civil society when, in the face of an uncivil society and an unaccountable state, minorities are left to protect and take care of their own members. Adding insult to injury, the state celebrates this abdication of its own responsibility as the triumph of civil society.

In a travesty of democracy, we have a situation where the state feels itself accountable to only one section of its citizens, the so-called "permanent majority" of Hindus. If minorities have a place in this new ethnically homogenous conception of the nation, it is as second-class citizens who have no rights and will merely be tolerated at the lowest rungs of the social, economic, and political hierarchy. They are expected to live by the rules set for them by the Hindus, who are the political majority by virtue of their demographic strength. In this game of numbers, polygamy, permitted under Muslim personal law, becomes a contentious issue for the Hindu right. It is falsely seen as leading to a disproportionate growth of the Muslim population which will then outnumber the Hindus in their own "homeland."

There is, in addition, a long record of nonaccountability of the state in the context of sectarian violence in India. Under public scrutiny and pressure from the press and civil liberties groups, the government has set up judicial enquiry commissions following all major riots. In addition to independent investigations and reports by civil liberties groups, these official commissions have submitted well-researched reports on, for example, the Delhi riots against Sikhs after Mrs. Gandhi's murder and the Bombay riots against Muslims after the destruction of the Babri mosque in Ayodhya by Hindu fanatics. However, despite the perpetrators (including local politicians, individual police officers, and civil servants) being named in these reports, no action has ever been taken against any of them. Neither individual nor collective political responsibility for any kind of human rights violations and violence directed at ethnic or religious minorities has ever been assigned. Based on this history, everybody knows that perpetrators, enjoying political patronage, will go unpunished and can continue to incite others and commit crimes against minorities with impunity. So that as civil liberties and human rights activists have realized, democracy is a necessary but by no means sufficient condition for state accountability. The institutionalization of these mechanisms of accountability is a slow and laborious process.

The long-term prospects worry me enormously. After talking to a lot of eyewitnesses to the looting and arson, I believe that the average age of those who committed these crimes was much younger than ever before in episodes of sectarian violence. The looters in Gujarat, many of whom had their mothers with them, were college-educated, middle-class boys, 20 to 25 years old. They often carried away the looted goods in cars parked nearby, cars driven by their fathers and husbands. This generation of youngsters has been brought up on a hatred of minorities: Muslims, Christians, Dalits or so-called "untouchable" castes. They have been taught history rewritten in the light of Hindu religious right-wing propaganda and disseminated through widely circulated pamphlets read and believed in urban middle-class homes. This generation of Gujarat youth has seen four major riots in the state against one or more minority groups. They have seen neighbors, relatives, and even their own parents looting, torching, and committing—or at least vociferously defending in public and in private—all kinds of violence against minorities. If they read newspapers, they have only read the regional Gujarati press with its consistently antiminority attitude and prejudices. The entire domestic and political socialization of a whole generation brought up on hatred and resentment of minorities has culminated in the kind of violence we have seen this time in Gujarat. And this is only the beginning of the story, I am afraid.

The high degree of middle-class participation in urban violence is only possible if you've had such a widespread socialization into this resentment. This was violence in which more than hatred was in play. We were told repeatedly in interviews that the Muslims had to be put in their place, meaning that they need to be taught that they are second-class citizens and they are going to stay that way. Putting Muslims in their place also meant destroying any economic competition that could stem from them, which is why all means of subsistence and livelihood for Muslims were destroyed. But for the very first time mosques, dargahs, and tombstones were razed to the ground. Within a couple of days there were either roads or small Hindu shrines built at these sites to erase every sign and memory of the demolition. Without state complicity or forethought and systematic planning, neither this kind of construction nor the singling out of Muslim shops and businesses for destruction could have been possible. The highly cynical political calculation behind this engineered violence is the speculation of an easy electoral victory for the BJP in Gujarat riding on the wave of Hindu support.[1]

Civil Society Organizations and Communal Violence

Aryeh Neier: I'm curious about what you think of the work of Ashutosh Varshney, the Indian sociologist. He argues that such violence has not taken place in communities divided between Hindus and Muslims where civil society organizations were formed across religious lines to deal with education or the availability of electric power or similar things that have nothing to do with ethnic or communal violence. He argues that, over the years, the communal violence in India has repeatedly arisen in cities like Ahmadabad, where these kinds of civil society organizations do not operate.

Shalini Randeria: It's a plausible thesis but it simplifies a complex story. For one, I am not sure which way the causal connection works. It may also be that in cities torn by religious animosity, no mixed civil society organizations have been able to develop or sustain themselves over the last few decades. So that we would be faced by a chicken and egg problem in relation to the Varshney thesis. Moreover, I feel

---

[1] When I said this in May 2002, I was hoping against hope that my pessimistic prediction would be proved wrong. The overwhelming victory for the BJP in the December elections in Gujarat capitalized on anti-Muslim sentiments. The government also successfully played on the widespread resentment among the Gujarati middle class against the condemnation of the pogroms in the rest of the country and especially in the national press. Its electoral rhetoric of "us" vs. "them" referred to not only Muslims as belonging to the latter category but also Christians, secularists, non-Gujaratis or "outsiders," all of those whom were felt to sympathize with the Muslims.

it underestimates the political forces at work, the ideological poisoning through school textbooks and so on, which prepares the ground for this kind of systematic violence. The modern civil society organizations he is talking about exist in most urban areas, and they are very much middle-class organizations. I don't think these organizations are a sufficient bulwark against the kind of communalization that has taken place in Gujarat in particular. Gujarat is the only area in India where, during the last five years, there has been a decline in per capita income. And yet the pattern of violence against minorities in various areas within the state differs significantly according to district. It is rather surprisingly the very opposite of what Varshney's study would lead us to expect. In the more industrialized, more urbanized, more "developed" districts and towns, with many more modern civil society organizations, there has been much greater violence against Muslims as compared to the less industrialized and so-called more "backward" areas where there is a greater continuity of older feudal structures and political culture. Taking his cue from Harvard Professor Robert Putnam, Varshney focuses too much on civic organizations to the neglect of political and economic and other cultural factors. I think there are many other variables, which we need to take into account in addition to the kinds of modern civil society organizations in order to explain the occurrence or nonoccurrence of sectarian violence.

Aryeh Neier: But part of his argument is that communal violence has repeatedly occurred in the same places over the last 50 years. You can essentially take eight cities or so, and they are the places where most of the communal violence has taken place. Other cities with a comparable Hindu-Muslim division have not had this kind of violence.

Shalini Randeria: But even in the cities prone to communal violence this is not a continuous affair. We need an explanation of the long years of communal harmony even in those cities that have periodically seen some of the worst violence. A focus on modern civic life alone is unable to explain this. I think that the nature and pattern of the violence are much more complex. Varshney's thesis, for example, cannot account for the emergence and robustness of civic associations with mixed Hindu-Muslim membership in some cities but not in others. Moreover, the present weakness of mixed membership trade unions in the textile industry of Ahmadabad, for example, is due to the decline of the entire industry and with it the once very strong labor union. But even before it declined, it was unable to prevent the 1969 Hindu-Muslim riots in the city. On the other hand, even in the absence of any modern civic organizations, there has been little history of communal violence in the villages of Gujarat. Curiously, West Bengal and Punjab—states where the worst communal carnage took place during the partition in 1947, so that memories of this violence are still alive among those who witnessed it and whose families suffered—have had among the fewest incidents of communal violence since then. Under what conditions is it possible to capitalize successfully on the politics of resentment against minorities of all kinds regardless of their numbers and political or economic strength?

Aryeh Neier: There was also the episode in, I think, about 1990, when a number of students burned themselves to death in protest against quotas or preferences. This was an astonishing set of events for me. I'd never heard of anything comparable any place else in the world.

Shalini Randeria: This was part of the so-called "antireservation" movement against quotas in public employment and institutions of higher education that reserve places for members of lower castes and so-called "untouchable" castes at the bottom of the caste hierarchy. The fact that the Indian constitution grants quotas and privileges to certain Hindu groups based on their traditional socially and educationally disadvantaged status has turned into a major grievance for upper-caste urban middle-class youth. To express their frustration, resentment, and fear of losing job opportunities, some of them immolated themselves in cities. They felt that the state is discriminating against its "majority" Hindu population by giving special concessions to "backward" or "untouchable" Hindu castes for political reasons.

At the time of this backlash, we as human rights activists sided with the Hindu minority communities under attack. And that was when in Gujarat, for example, we first burnt our bridges with the upper caste/middle class most of us come from. The fact that in every successive riot against Muslims and Christians the small community of human rights activists, which is also a secular one, upheld minority rights only served to increase the gulf. Today many of the Hindu lower castes whose rights to quotas we vociferously defended are as virulently anti-Muslim as the upper castes. A Hindu unity across the caste divide has been formed throughout the last couple of decades by mobilizing against Muslims and then Christians as the "Other." We need to find a language to talk to ordinary Hindus and to build bridges with Muslim organizations.

Samantha Power: I have a question about the one sliver of good news in your entire depressing account. And this was what you said about the press not exacerbating things, not polarizing the communities. What you see accompanying most cases of genocide and atrocity is that the press gets involved and serves the polarization and demonization process. In your account, is the press lying low for the same reasons you described, the kind of affirmative action reasons? Or does the press want to be a stabilizing force, a defusing force?

Shalini Randeria: This is very hard to tell. On the affirmative action issue in the 1980s, on which I've worked for many years both as a scholar and as an activist, the press has not always been supportive. The national press with its indisputably higher quality of journalism has always been much more balanced, even though it was by and large against the lower castes on the issue of quotas. The Gujarati press has been particularly partisan and vicious in its attacks against the Dalits or "untouchable" castes and has incited violence against them by its highly contentious reports. Its bias against Muslim and Christian minorities is equally well known. This time, for the first time, several Gujarati newspapers have not been as irresponsible or even polarizing. I don't quite know why. The really cynical explanation is that the election calculus of the newspaper owners is playing a part in restraining them. And even the highly communalized and powerful Hindu business community in Gujarat tired of the violence after a few days of suffering enormous economic losses.

The national English language press and especially television have always been less biased, more even-handed on the Hindu-Muslim question. The pressure on the federal government from the national press and especially from television stations in Delhi was very helpful in stemming the violence in Gujarat. The rioters mobilized and coordinated their activities very well using mobile phones and other devices. But the live coverage, the first time around on television in India, brought into all middle-class urban homes these images of police passivity in the face of frenzied looting by well-dressed middle-class crowds.

Joost Hiltermann: Samantha, you spoke about the United States government and prevention of genocide. It's a very depressing story, too, because this is a record of nonintervention in cases of genocide. What would it take for the United States to turn its bureaucracy around? Could you do it through value-based arguments? Or can you somehow press for interest-based arguments? And would these arguments point out that, over the long term, it is in your interest to observe human rights?

Bosnia and Kosovo: Politics and a President's Legacy

Samantha Power: I'll address this descriptively, in terms of looking back. Then I'll get to how I perceive things going forward. And I'll leave aside discussing whether or not a particular response escalates to military intervention.

The only time you see a meaningful political response, an actual inclusion of genocide in the American foreign-policy calculus, is when you have some traditional interest invoked. This could be a short-term domestic political interest, which is what you had in the case of Bosnia in the summer of 1995. What it took to secure military intervention was an alteration of the cost-benefit calculus, making the risks of nonintervention—non-military intervention or military nonintervention—for Bill Clinton greater than the risks of involvement. The risks diminished after the Croatian army had vanquished the Serbs in Croatia; the threat posed by the Serbs diminished. Bob Dole and a number of senators, combined with grassroots and grasstops political pressure, had an effect. There was editorial support for intervention. Congress voted to lift the arms embargo against the Muslims in late July or early August of 1995. This put President Clinton in a position where he was facing the utterly unenviable prospect of getting militarily involved in order to extract European peacekeepers—because the Europeans had said if the arms embargo were lifted, they were going to get out of there. Suddenly, Clinton said, "Oh, my God. I'm going to have to send U.S. troops to aid a European withdrawal and Muslims are going to be throwing themselves in front of tanks," pleading with the peacekeepers to stay. So that was a practical outcome of the efforts by Dole and other people.

The potential political cost was even greater. There was the impression that foreign policy was being made on Capitol Hill by a Senate majority leader, a Republican, a future presidential challenger. It was humiliating. The inside story of those negotiations in late July and early August really does seem to confirm that what motivated him was not mere values, which he could have invoked all along. There certainly was some added force from the images of Srebrenica and some of David's great reporting and that of other journalists. This made the values element more powerful, or made it felt more viscerally. But the values element was never going to be sufficient on its own.

What was added to the mix was political interest, not in the sense of strategic interest even. It wasn't regional spillover or even NATO credibility, though, again, these factors were at the margins. It was raw political calculus. So that's the descriptive account of the one case where you've actually seen a military intervention.

Kosovo was quite similar in that you got a sense that Clinton's political legacy was at stake. You have Milosevic as a repeat offender, so the alibis that one invokes, or the story one tells oneself about political processes and negotiation being the root to political solution—alibis often invoked in the case of genocide where negotiation and neutrality can actually abet atrocity—had by then melted away. It was just too much of the same guy for too long. Also there were personal commitments on a higher level to wiping the egg off their chins. Madeleine Albright took Warren

Christopher's place. Sandy Berger took Tony Lake's place. And these were people who were prepared to put more on the line and who felt like they had been around this block too many times. Again, it was not merely the sight of Albanians hugging the hillside. You've got to have the nexus.

So where does this leave us in terms of how to go forward?

It seems to me that the American response to genocide could change in one of several ways. One is leadership. Let's say we had a president who did not just trek up to the Holocaust Museum and say, "Never again." Let's say we had a president who came into office on the heels of a genocide that he or she had been pissed off about and decided that such a thing would not happen on his or her watch. Or let's say we had a president who went to Gujarat and saw what was happening and had some personal connection with atrocities and entered office and issued presidential directives, made public speeches, did contingency military planning, and signaled the bureaucracy that, at a minimum, potential genocides must generate robust, high-level diplomatic and economic involvement.

Let's say this president declared that the U.S. would do everything it could along the continuum of intervention, and when it came to the red zone of military intervention, we would have a public debate. One can't, of course, commit to invading Russia to stop some imminent genocide in Chechnya. But one can certainly do a lot of things along the continuum and be creative in giving this crime the priority it deserves. So you can imagine, at least, a president doing that. I have a hard time imagining the possibility as reality, but anyway, it's a possibility. "It's leadership, stupid." He or she could do it for the simple reason that it is moral, that genocide is simply wrong. Or he or she could look back at the record of the last couple of decades and say, "My God, when genocide happens and we allow it to happen, it comes back to bite us. When we allowed the arms embargo to be imposed against Yugoslavia, affecting the Muslims more than anyone else, wow, Al Qaeda got in there and used Bosnia as a training base. And you know, when we allowed Muslims to die, they became radicalized. Muslims half way around the world are still talking about how we let them die. When we allowed Saddam to use chemical weapons against the Kurds and to destroy them, he took it as a signal that he could also use chemical weapons against anybody else he chose, to invade Kuwait, and ultimately to be a source of great instability in a region that was actually meaningful to us and a great source of terror still to this day. It's strange how this backlash keeps happening."

Now the problem with this interest-based approach, of course, is Rwanda and Burundi and other cases where we don't care about the regions into which the genocide spills. Although human rights groups are doing everything in their power to find an Al Qaeda connection to every country in Africa, they're not succeeding generally. But in Sierra Leone they found a connection. So if merely chopping off hands isn't enough to move you, you'll be relieved to know that in fact bin Laden laundered his money through conflict diamonds.

Then, finally, there is the way it happened in Bosnia. The pressure placed on our leaders has to affect the calculus. You can affect the calculus by naming names and spoiling reputations after the fact. You can hope this makes policymakers worry that they're going to end up being named as a bystander. This is a new worry, because there hasn't been much tracking of bystanding at least on the American side. Or you could apply this pressure in real time, somehow mobilizing a sense that the country or leader will pay a price either strategically, in the Saddam or bin Laden example, or politically, in the Dole-Clinton example.

It took three and a half years to get that kind of intervention in Bosnia. I think we can look back more appreciatively on what at the time seemed like meaningless soft sanctions. I've concluded that noise gets you the soft sanctions, and domestic political or strategic risk can get you a meaningful military intervention. Even though we felt that the noise from Bosnia was very ineffective, you can imagine what that country would have looked like if we'd actually shut down entirely and if there had been no U.S. sanctions and no condemnations, if we had just looked away as we did for every other case. I think it probably would have been much worse for Bosnia.

Haiti and Somalia: More on the Politics of Intervention

Aryeh Neier: I want to supplement these comments. First, just to support the idea that the political calculus is what has been determinative, I will cite two examples of military intervention where the abuses that took place didn't rise to the level of genocide. One would be Haiti, and the other would be Somalia.

The reason for the military intervention in Haiti was that after two and a half or three years of military rule in Haiti, with about 3,000 killings by the military during that period, you had a flotilla of small boats bringing Haitian refugees to the United States. They were coming to Florida. They were resented in Florida. The question of where Florida's electoral votes would go became very important to the Clinton administration. The Clinton administration couldn't very well adopt the measures taken by the Bush and Reagan administrations. Reagan had the Haitian boats stopped at sea, and the Haitians were repatriated to Haiti. Clinton had criticized this policy during his electoral campaign in 1992. On this particular issue, he also faced a revolt from the Congressional Black Caucus, a group that hasn't thrown its weight around at all on human rights issues—if anything, it has been counterproductive on human rights issues. The Black Caucus opposed interdiction. Given the slight majority that Clinton had in the House of Representatives at that time, he needed the Congressional Black Caucus. Since he couldn't re-impose interdiction, the only way he could keep the Haitians from coming to Florida and costing him Florida's electoral votes in the next election, was to invade Haiti. This, I would say, was the principal political factor in the decision to invade Haiti. It sounds bizarre, but it was the politics of that moment.

Then there was Somalia. In a way, Somalia got divorced from political calculations because the senior Bush had been under attack by Clinton for not paying attention to domestic issues, for focusing on foreign policy. So, during the 1992 electoral campaign, Bush's hands were tied in terms of dealing with foreign issues, because he had to focus on domestic issues. You remember. The slogan during the electoral campaign was "It's the economy, stupid." Bush was losing because of the economy. He couldn't deal with Somalia or Bosnia. Eventually, his defeat in the first week of November in 1992 liberated Bush. He announced the sending of U.S. troops to Somalia at Thanksgiving about two weeks later. He was a lame-duck president until January 20. He had both Bosnia and Somalia on the agenda, and his advisors said Somalia would be easier. The slogan was "We do deserts, not mountains." Bush did not want to go out having done nothing about at least one of these great calamities underway at that time. Since Somalia was easier, he sent troops into Somalia.

Now that I have demonstrated my own cynicism about the way these things have taken place, I'll give my view of what is needed to make the United States more responsive to genocide. This is something at least as difficult as anything else that one could propose as a way of changing the way the United States responds. It essentially requires dealing with the unilateralism of the United States. As long as the United States is completely distrustful of multilateral intervention, it is going to be virtually impossible to get the United States to respond to genocide. There is always going to be the issue of why the United States should be the country to respond. On the other hand, if there were a commitment to multilateralism, a sharing of responsibility, there would be a much greater possibility of intervention.

As a result of Kosovo, American mistrust of multilateralism now extends to NATO. There are countries in this region still trying to join NATO, not knowing that NATO is actually finished. NATO is finished, because the United States was very annoyed by the restrictions that came out of multilateral decision making with respect to Kosovo. If you remember, right after September 11, NATO adopted a resolution saying that an attack on one is an attack on all, in effect offering NATO to conduct the war in Afghanistan. The United States wanted nothing to do with this offer because of the Kosovo experience. The United States decided to run the war. Other countries could contribute, but the United States would run the war. It wouldn't be NATO running the war.

I think it would be very difficult to have a decision made with respect to Kosovo if Kosovo came up again, because of the new United States hostility to NATO.

When I think of multilateral responses, I think of East Timor. Were it not for the availability of Australian troops, there would not have been an international military intervention in East Timor. The United States was ready to provide logistical support to the Australians, but it would not have been ready to provide troops to go into East Timor. There has been discussion of an African Rapid Reaction Force of African troops that would intervene in a conflict in Africa. The United States would provide logistical support. And although one could criticize the manner in which Nigeria intervened in Liberia and Sierra Leone, on the whole, it was a good thing that Nigeria did intervene in these conflicts. The Nigerian troops themselves committed a lot of abuses. But if you assume that it's not going to be the United States sending troops into Liberia or Sierra Leone, that it has to be African troops, then really what you require is an American commitment to multilateralism for any such intervention to take place.

Right now, the attitude in the United States is that Europe is getting a free ride, that Europe is not spending anything on defense. American expenditures on defense are a significant multiple of what Europe spends even though the economy of the European Union is roughly comparable in size to the economy of the United States. So Europe is getting a free ride. They depend on us for military security. We are being asked to carry the burden, and the United States won't respond to genocide somewhere unless there is some burden sharing.

The American commitment to unilateralism, and its antagonism toward multilateralism, prevents any such burden sharing from taking place. So, in my view, any attempt to deal with the willingness of the United States to respond to genocide has to focus first and foremost on overcoming this unilateralism that is stronger under this administration than under any previous administration.

Samantha Power: I just want to make one point to bring the discussion back to Gujarat. I think it's very important not to limit this discussion to what to do about genocide. We're not going to intervene militarily in Gujarat, of course. But there is a lot more that we might be doing preventatively if genocide was higher on our list of priorities. This is not to say Gujarat is experiencing genocide now. But there are massacres that seem to be occurring along with systematic, ethnically targeted economic destruction. What is happening is enough to raise red flags and to warrant at least assistant-secretary-level attention. It isn't getting any attention, because it's not a priority. Part of the many downsides to the war on terrorism is that our resources are directed toward Jenin and toward Afghanistan and away from Gujarat. So the nongovernmental actors who might have some capacity to be agenda-shapers in this area are themselves distracted.

I think it's important to think creatively and ask what steps could be taken to put pressure on the central government or to invest in civil society.

Shalini Randeria: Let me just add a final comment. September 11 and the war on terrorism plays a role in aggravating this whole climate of targeting Muslims as fanatics, fundamentalists, and terrorists. Supposedly the pogrom against Muslims in Gujarat started as a spontaneous reaction to the burning by a crowd of Muslims of the train carriages carrying Hindu right-wing activists. The whole image of the Muslim as inherently prone to irrational violence, as a terrorist, is something that has taken on a global dimension. The Hindu right-wing organizations in Gujarat which are behind the pogroms know that not only will the regional and the federal governments protect them, but the entire Western media and public opinion in a sense shares in their perception of the Muslims as perpetrators of violence who deserve a heavy-handed response. At this point in time, it is possible to get away with a lot more violence against Muslims with impunity than was possible earlier. Not that the Indian government has been particularly sensitive to international condemnation or pressure with regard to its poor record of human rights violations. But it can bank on the fact that even censure is unlikely now. And like many other religious diasporas, the Hindu diaspora in the United Kingdom and United States has been the financial backbone of many of these Hindu right-wing organizations in India and abroad.

IV.

Intervention, Interference, and Inaction

Moderator: *Aryeh Neier*
Speaker: *Bill Berkeley*
Comments: *Sonja Licht*, board member and former president,
Fund for an Open Society-Serbia

Aryeh Neier: I once heard Sonja Licht say that the foundation in Yugoslavia started with a united country, and then kept covering a smaller and smaller territory as the country divided. She assumed that at some point the foundation would deal with the area circumscribed by, I think, the No. 2 tramline in Belgrade. At any rate, the diminishing size of the territory doesn't diminish Sonja's significance as a leader of efforts to promote open society in the Balkans and far more broadly.

Bill Berkeley: I will talk about ethnic conflict and American foreign policy. I'll focus primarily on Africa, the area I know best.

I thought that I would pick up on where Samantha Power left off with her discussion of the Clinton administration's failure to intervene in Rwanda in 1994. I was in Rwanda while the massacres were going on. My experience was something like David's description of his experience in Israel. On the ground, it's hard to know what the rest of the world is thinking and how the rest of the world is reacting. But I remember vividly that while I was in Rwanda—and it was an extremely ugly business, I assure you—it never even occurred to me that the United States would intervene constructively.

The first reason for this is that less than a year earlier the Somalia fiasco had occurred and given the Clinton administration an extreme dose of reluctance to intervene anywhere in Africa. But there is a broader reason that intervention was the furthest thing from my mind. By the time I was in Rwanda in 1994, I had been traveling back and forth to Africa for nearly a decade, and I had covered any number of other conflicts. I learned that the history of American involvement in Africa, far from being one of omission and failure to intervene constructively, was quite the opposite. It was a history of intervening destructively.

I think most Americans, when they think of Africa, think of its problems as remote from our experience and our interests. In fact, quite the opposite is the case. America has been deeply involved in Africa for most of the last century, both diplomatically and economically.

My own most recent experience, prior to the genocide in Rwanda in 1994, had been in Liberia, a country where America had much stronger ties than it had with Rwanda. U.S. involvement with the Liberian government goes back to the 19th century. The Voice of America broadcasts from Liberia, from a station in Monrovia, which was named after an American president. The next largest city, Buchanan, is also named after an American president. The Liberian flag is modeled after the American flag. A professor at Harvard Law School drew up the Liberian constitution. The CIA had its main station for all of sub-Saharan Africa in the embassy in Monrovia. Firestone operated the world's largest rubber plantation in Liberia. At the time of the military dictatorship of Samuel Doe in the 1980s, the United States was paying a third of Liberia's national budget. It had contributed half a billion dollars in military aid to Samuel Doe's army.

When Liberia descended into civil war in 1990–a war every bit as brutal as Rwanda's, albeit spread out over a longer period–about 10 percent of the country's population was murdered. When that war began and Liberians looked to the United States to intervene, American warships settled off the coast of Monrovia to evacuate Americans but otherwise declined to intervene. This was, really, the pattern of America's involvement across Africa.

So, by 1994, when Rwanda descended into barbarism, the possibility of America intervening was the last thing on my mind. I will quote a former colleague of mine on the editorial board of the *New York Times*, Karl Meyer, who once referred to America's involvement in places like Liberia as the Buchanan strain of American foreign policy. And by this he meant not the politician Pat Buchanan, but Tom and Daisy Buchanan, F. Scott Fitzgerald's careless couple in *The Great Gatsby*, who, to quote from the book, "smashed up things and creatures and then retreated back into their money... and let other people clean up the mess they had made." This is a really apt description of what happened in Liberia and elsewhere in Africa.

Interestingly, Karl Meyer was referring to American policy in Afghanistan. And the truth is there are many parallels between Africa and Afghanistan. It's not a coincidence, as Samantha joked, that Africans are trying as hard as they can to find bin Laden connections in order to make Africa relevant. In fact, there are many bin Laden connections in Africa. Bin Laden built his Al Qaeda network in Sudan, not just because of its National Islamic Front, which has dominated Sudan for the last decade, but because Sudan, like Afghanistan, is a permanent war zone. Sudan has, among other things, the kind of black market economy that a terrorist organization like Al Qaeda depends upon and thrives in.

Demystifying Ethnic Conflict in Africa

But let me step back and summarize the basic argument of my book. It helps explain why America's role in Africa has been so important historically. My book is an attempt to demystify ethnic conflict, to explain for American readers why Africans have been killing each other in large numbers for the last decade. It focuses on a half dozen countries: Liberia; Zaire under Mobutu; South Africa in the last decade of apartheid; Sudan; Uganda; and Rwanda. These are conflicts in which tens of thousands of civilians have been murdered. Many Americans looking at these conflicts from afar imagine that they have their roots in ancient hatreds. They seem inscrutable. People seem to be behaving in ways that are "senseless." This is a great word, "senseless." It appears again and again in the American press, even in the *Times*. The fact is, however, that these conflicts are anything but senseless. People are behaving rationally. They're making rational calculations in their own self-interest. Some people are benefiting. They're acquiring power. Africans and their business partners near and far are acquiring great riches.

My basic argument is that these conflicts are not exotic. There is a recognizable logic to them. People are killing each other in Africa for the same reason people have killed each other in large numbers in all parts of the world throughout all of history. Ethnic conflict in Africa is a product of tyranny. Tyrants and aspiring tyrants use ethnic conflict as a means to acquire and hold onto power. Their tactics are similar to what we've seen in the Balkans and elsewhere in the last decade: propaganda, the mobilization of ethnically based militias, the magnification of existing grievances and prejudices, the manipulation and exploitation of history. All of these familiar tactics that we know from other parts of the world are very much in evidence in all of the conflicts that I'm familiar with in Africa.

As I mentioned earlier, it is now well established that the Rwanda genocide was state-orchestrated. The same is true in all of these other conflicts. And as bad as Rwanda was, and it was and remains extremely bad, I'm here to tell you that all of these conflicts are bad. They all have analogous sources, not just in the immediate sense of tyrants seeking to acquire and hold onto power now. But, just as importantly, they have at least a century-long history of tyranny, and specifically racial tyranny:

- Liberia, a century and a half of domination by the Americo-Liberians, the descendants of freed American slaves who dominated a vast majority of indigenous inhabitants through tactics of coercion;
- Sudan, a history of Arab domination of black African southern Sudanese and roots dating back to the Arab slave trade;

- Uganda, a history of British colonial rule;
- Zaire, Rwanda, a history of Belgian colonial rule;
- South Africa, a history of British colonial rule and apartheid.

The legacies of racial tyranny in Africa have outlasted the demise of the systems they were designed to preserve. I will draw your attention to a very important legacy you may not be familiar with: the system of indirect rule. It's a basic lesson of the history of tyranny in Africa, as elsewhere. Small minorities of whites or other minorities can't dominate vast majorities indefinitely merely by cracking heads. They need to manipulate what's inside them. They need to find collaborators, indigenous folks willing to do their dirty work for them. The classic example is Rwanda. Historically in Rwanda, the Tutsis, the victims of genocide in 1994, played the collaborator role. And this legacy of collaboration was used and magnified and exploited by the Hutu military leadership in Rwanda as a means of mobilizing the Hutu masses to defend that military leadership.

So, ethnic conflict is a legacy of tyranny and a tactic of tyranny. How does America play into that?

Historically, as most of you know, Americans have embraced, financed, armed, and legitimized tyrants for strategic interests, notably during the Cold War, and also for economic interests.

Let me just briefly highlight some economic interests, since many Americans are not familiar with them. A particularly vivid example is Firestone in Liberia. In league with the Americo-Liberian oligarchy, Firestone operated the world's largest rubber plantation in Liberia for the better part of the last century. In effect, the Americo-Liberian oligarchy, comprising maybe 2 or 3 percent of Liberia's population over the last century, dominated a vast indigenous population through a combination of coercion and co-optation. But they needed financing, and Firestone provided it. Firestone bankrolled the Americo-Liberian dictatorship for most of the last century and continued to do so once Samuel Doe seized power in 1980.

Another vivid example is Folgers coffee in Burundi. An earlier genocide, one most of you are probably not familiar with, occurred in 1972 in Burundi. The Tutsi-dominated army murdered about 100,000 to 200,000 Burundian Hutus. It was a horrific genocide in its own right. But it also helps explain some of the background of what occurred in Rwanda two decades later. At the time of the Burundian genocide in 1972, Folgers coffee was responsible for 65 percent of Burundi's foreign exchange. As the largest business in Burundi, it played an important role in bankrolling Burundi's Tutsi-dominated military dictatorship.

Another example: In Zaire, Maurice Tempelsman, a very important diamond trader, played a role, together with Lebanese businessmen, in bankrolling Mobutu

Sese Seko's military dictatorship. So America is by no means alone in this regard. Folks from all over the world, from Europe, the Middle East, and beyond, as well as Africans themselves, have played important roles in financing military dictatorship in Africa.

The dictators in turn played dirty to hold onto power. This was particularly true during the immediate aftermath of the Cold War, when strategic backing for dictatorships began to disappear and the props were kicked out from under dictators all across the continent. Aspiring tyrants, notably Charles Taylor, seeing Samuel Doe with his back against the wall, likewise played the ethnic card in order to acquire power.

So we have America deeply involved in Liberia with Samuel Doe, in Zaire with Mobutu, and in Sudan, in the early 80s, with Jaafar Nimeiry, who was that country's head of state at the beginning of its civil war. A reminder: Sudan has been at war now for 18 years and running. More than two million southern Sudanese have died in this war, mostly from starvation and disease. The war was initiated by Jaafar Nimeiry, who was our man in Sudan. Mohammed Siad Barre was our man in Somalia. We basically traded for him with the Soviet Union in the late 1970s in exchange for the Ethiopian dictator, Mengistu Haile Miriam, who became a Soviet client.

Overwhelmingly, America's approach to Africa during the Cold War was dominated by strategic considerations, by our competition with the Soviet Union, which was really the only consideration of American policymakers. I single out Chester Crocker in my book. I mentioned him earlier and quoted him making no apologies for his own policies in Africa. But it is very important to emphasize that Chester Crocker—although he was a particularly controversial figure, with the kind of personality that tends to attract controversy—was by no means exceptional. He was typical of American policymakers in Democratic administrations as well as in Republican administrations throughout the Cold War, dating back to the Eisenhower administration, and including the Kennedy administration, which was in power at the time that Mobutu seized power in Zaire.

So, ethnic conflict is a tactic of tyranny. The United States has been a backer of tyranny historically. And tyrants are playing the ethnic card as a means of acquiring and holding on to power.

Ethnicity in Africa is really no different than it is in other parts of the world. There is nothing exotic about it. We tend to use the word "tribe" to describe ethnic groups in Africa. This word is often used for ethnic groups in Afghanistan as well. My own experience has shown me that tribes in Africa are ethnic groups like ethnic groups across the globe. They are malleable. Their identities have evolved and changed over time. Most ethnic groups in Africa live side by side in peace. Historically, ethnicity has been, in overwhelmingly rural societies, a source of social services and protection, particularly in the absence of legitimate institutions of law and accountability. This absence itself is another legacy of colonial rule in Africa. In the absence of legitimate police institutions, legitimate courts, legitimate armies, ethnicity has been a source of protection. And that protective role in Africa has particular resonance dating back to the slave trade.

The historian Basil Davidson, perhaps Britain's preeminent historian of Africa, has written interestingly on the role of ethnic groups and their formation for purposes of protection against slave raiding beginning in the 15th and 16th centuries. So ethnicity is a source of protection, a means of mobilization, and, as it is elsewhere across the globe, a source of legitimacy for political leaders and aspiring political leaders who otherwise lack any form of political legitimacy.

A U.S. History of Intervening Destructively

I also want to talk about the United States and the political context in which these policies have been pursued historically. I think we all agreed earlier that U.S. administrations have more recently declined to intervene in Africa. Historically, however, to the extent that we have intervened, we've intervened destructively. We've done so, for the most part, because the American public has paid little or no attention at all to what Americans are doing in Africa.

Obviously, with political Cold War calculations predominant in Washington, policymakers were always able to rationalize policies that had destructive consequences for Africans as part of the larger Cold War strategic competition with the Soviets. Chester Crocker and others whom I interviewed expressed no regrets whatsoever about our conduct in Africa during the Cold War. In a larger sense, in their eyes, our competition with the Soviets was a legitimate competition. Our alternatives, in the view of many policymakers, were extremely limited. The Cold War provided a kind of inoculation from any moral considerations that might have intervened.

But there are other considerations as well. They stem from America's own unresolved history of race relations. I would like to identify two. One, in my experience, is a kind of unwitting collusion between left and right in America vis-à-vis Africa. This collusion persists to this day. On the right, there is a view of Africa that I would characterize as racist. It is the view that Africans are unfit to govern themselves, that a 28-year-old, semiliterate master sergeant like Samuel Doe was as good a business partner as we might find in Africa, that we were unlikely to find any more enlightened leaders. You hear this from many people on the right, sometimes explicitly and sometimes not. Over the years, I've received letters from readers responding to what

I've written about black African military dictators. These letters have said, "What do you expect? Africans are unfit to govern themselves." So I believe racism plays a role—sometimes subtly, sometimes not—in helping to rationalize our propping up of unsavory black African leaders.

On the left in the United States—including African Americans—there is, for various reasons, an unwillingness to publicize the crimes of African dictators or to criticize America's alliances with African dictators. Perhaps understandably, there is a concern about perpetuating racial stereotypes, a concern that white Americans would misunderstand such criticisms. As a journalist who began writing about Africa in 1984, I can tell you that the number of African Americans who have been in the forefront of documenting human rights abuses in Africa, for example, is extremely limited.

This unwitting collusion between right and left has made it possible for America and its diplomats, year after year, to go up before Congress and explain away the abuses of folks like Doe and Mobutu and Siad Barre. The one exception was South Africa. With apartheid, the crimes were easy to understand, the injustices flagrant and readily identified. In the 1980s, African Americans took the lead in protesting the abuses of apartheid and ultimately protesting the Reagan Administration's implicit alliance with the apartheid regime. Chester Crocker, the assistant secretary of state, came under the most withering criticism from, among others, African Americans, who understood all too readily what apartheid was all about. But there really was no analogous movement in the United States to protest the crimes of some of Africa's black tyrannies.

I think the press has played a role in enabling Washington to cozy up to some of these bad actors. There have been some great American journalists in Africa over the years. Joe Lelyveld, who was executive editor of the *New York Times* until recently, was a great correspondent in South Africa. Blaine Harden, formerly of the *Washington Post*, one of the all-time great correspondents, wrote eloquently about Africa. But in my own experience, over a period of 15 years, by and large, American press coverage of Africa has been overwhelmingly crisis-dominated, focusing on the symptoms of conflict rather than on the causes. Explications of Africa's history have been simplistic and abbreviated and have overwhelmingly emphasized ancient hatreds and exotic tribal animosities. Americans perceive Africa as an unmitigated mass of pathetic and defenseless victims. Little understanding emerges of who is actually responsible for these conflicts, why people are behaving the way they are, and who is benefiting.

Ethnic conflict is a form of organized crime. In Africa, as elsewhere, people are making money from these conflicts, acquiring power and loot. Africa is a continent of enormous resources. We all know now about the diamonds. But there is also iron, copper, timber, gold, and lumber. All of these are resources that have, historically, attracted raiders and predators from near and far.

This brings me to the nature of these wars over the last decade. As the major Cold War powers have withdrawn their support for tyrants and rebel movements in Africa, organized criminal syndicates have moved in to fill that void. Smugglers of diamonds and weapons are playing a very important role now across the continent. Perhaps the most important weapons smuggler in Africa is a man named Victor Bout, a former Russian air force pilot and KGB officer from Tajikistan who, until very recently, operated out of the United Arab Emirates. Bout smuggled weapons primarily from Romania and Bulgaria and had allies from Lebanon, Israel, Kenya, Russia, Belgium, and the United States. They form a vast congregation of mafiosi preying on the war zones of west, central, and southern Africa.

Just to bring you up to date on the administrations of Clinton and Bush, I will again highlight the history of American involvement in Africa. In my own experience, the policy alternatives are not obvious. Even the most enlightened policies don't necessarily yield favorable results.

New African Leaders, Same Armed Conflicts

The Clinton administration came in 1993, after the Cold War. One might have hoped that without Cold War considerations dominating American policy, more enlightened policies might have been tried. Indeed, the Clinton administration brought in some of my old friends, people I considered to be enlightened and thoughtful. John Prendergast, someone with whom I spent Christmas Eve in Juba in south Sudan in 1988, rose to become Clinton's Africa hand on the National Security Council. Gayle Smith, an old NGO hand in the horn of Africa, was also there. These were good people, with good intentions. Their misgivings about the Reagan administration were very much akin to my own. They pursued what they viewed as fundamentally different approaches to Africa.

They embraced what they called a new generation of African leaders, folks like Yoweri Museveni in Uganda, Paul Kagame in Rwanda, and the horn of Africa's two heads of state. Clinton traveled to Africa in 1998. He spent more time in Africa than any American leader in history. He spoke of an African renaissance and of America's renewed interest in investment in Africa. There was much talk of what Clinton called "African solutions to African problems."

Many people hoped that Clinton's policies would be favorable. But within a matter of weeks after Clinton had traveled to Africa and embraced this so-called new generation of African leaders, all of them fell into warfare with each other. A ruinous war erupted between Ethiopia and Eritrea. It included trench warfare akin to the fighting in Europe during World War I. Perhaps 100,000 conscripts were killed within a few years. In Congo-Zaire, not one, but two wars unfolded. The violence was unleashed initially to bring down Mobutu. This was, seemingly, an enlightened goal in itself. But Congo has been at war ever since.

I think the Clinton folks learned that simply choosing men who seem to be more-enlightened and better-intentioned leaders will not, by itself, solve Africa's problems. The continent is suffering from enormously complicated problems that, in my view, have their roots not just in a nefarious cast of characters but in the institutional context in which certain kinds of characters excel. These newly embraced leaders, like Museveni and Kagame, are educated and articulate. They talk a good game. But, in fact, they acquired power by besting their adversaries at their own game, by being better at armed struggle than the men they overthrew. The Clinton administration failed to appreciate that embracing these kinds of folks simply empowered them to operate according to the same set of rules by which they had acquired power. I wouldn't hold the Clinton folks accountable for actually provoking armed conflict. But, during its eight years, the Clinton administration had little success in bringing armed conflict to an end.

The Bush administration is preoccupied with terrorism. I would like to end with the example of Sudan to highlight how important the political context in the United States is in driving American foreign policy in Africa. As I mentioned, Al Qaeda built the National Islamic Front in Sudan, just about as bad an outfit as you can find on earth. Like Al Qaeda, it is a kind of front organization—a hybrid of true believers in Islamist theocracy on the one hand and, on the other, gangsters exploiting and extracting wealth from Sudan at a cost of millions of lives. Bin Laden operated in Sudan for five years. Sudan's government has abundant intelligence on Al Qaeda, on its finances and business operations around the world. So there has been much concern that, after September 11, the Bush administration would turn a blind eye to the nefarious nature of the National Islamic Front and embrace Sudan as a potential ally in the war against terrorism.

But Sudan's behavior has been so bad—it stands accused of slavery and genocide, of wholesale state terror in which thousands of people have been tortured and two million have died—Sudan is so bad that it has acquired a broad array of vigorous opponents, even in the United States, from the Congressional Black Caucus, motivated by reports of slavery, to the evangelical Christian right, concerned about the persecution of Sudanese Christians by the Arab-dominated north. The Christian right is an important political base for the Bush administration. In a closely contested race, the Congressional Black Caucus can play a role. So the Bush administration, even if it might have wished to embrace the Sudanese government, has refrained from doing so because of political constraints in the United States. This is a rare instance in which the American public has actually played a role in American policy in Africa with beneficial results.

Aryeh Neier: When you referred to the fact that the wars in Africa are not senseless, I remembered a comment by another journalist who has covered Africa. Lindsay Hilson said that she found herself writing that the various conflicts she covered were chaotic before she realized that she didn't know what was going on and that this was the reason she thought they were chaotic.

Sonja, although you focus on the Balkans and not on Africa, you may have recognized a few parallels between them.

Sonja Licht: While listening to Bill, I found myself in a dilemma. It is, for me, an ongoing dilemma. Am I a witness or an analyst? We, in Yugoslavia, lived through everything: inaction, interference, intervention. All this was happening to us. Yet at the same time, we were forced to think about and analyze the situation in which we found ourselves. We had to ask what is happening and how it is appropriate to act in such a context.

I cannot resolve my dilemma. But I am terribly sorry Bill was not in Moscow in May 1990, at the first official meeting organized in Russia by the Helsinki Federation and Helsinki Watch on the issues of human rights in Russia and the region. At one point, a number of us from the Balkans, including some Romanians, were trying to understand how human rights organizations should approach the danger of ethnic conflict, which was casting its shadow over the entire region. The answer we came up with at that time was that we could not deal with it. We were used to dealing with governments, with one-party states. We simply could not deal with ethnic conflicts, because they had been generated almost always by different forces and not necessarily by the governments.

Of course, these same human rights organizations started dealing with ethnic conflict later on. And I don't think anything very crucial would have changed in the course of events after 1990 even if we had known how to approach ethnic conflicts and locate their role in major abuses of human rights.

I strongly believe that we have a serious responsibility, in the context of globalization, to consider the possibility of knowledge of global affairs. I do not believe it is possible to globalize this world in the way we would like to without seriously trying to explore the possibilities of knowledge.

One of the most important problems concerning the role of the United States in the Balkans and other regions in conflict is what it means to be the first global power. I understand that in Washington and other places there is a sense of great pride that the United States is the first and only global power. But I don't perceive enough understanding of the responsibility this position implies. What kind of leadership skills should this global power develop parallel with its sense of pride?

A Lack of Preventive Action in the Balkans and Elsewhere

In the Balkans, we saw the United States in several different stages. What bothers me most nowadays, however, is not inaction, interference, or intervention. What bothers me is the lack of preventive action and the understanding that preventive action or preventive diplomacy was the proper course to take in the Balkans.

I do not see any readiness for preventive action in other places either. As we watch the Middle East, we are also watching the United States as it thinks about how to leave the Balkans. A few weeks ago in Washington, I participated in a debate about how fast the United States should leave. Should it be immediately? How fast should the Europeans take over? In the region, there are concerns that a quick departure of the United States will create a void, because the Europeans are coming in very slowly.

These discussions are going on at the same time as Secretary of State Colin Powell is negotiating with Sharon and Arafat, promising them, as far as I understand it, a long-standing U.S. involvement after the Arab-Israeli conflict is settled. My question is this: If the United States is so intent on leaving the Balkans now, why would the people in the Middle East believe the United States will follow a different course of action there? Why would they believe that the United States will remain until there is sustainable peace and stability in that region?

These are not the only cases we can analyze. But I know my case best. This is why I want to state my case, our case. On the one hand, there was a lack of preventive action. With this in mind, I'd like to tell you about a few of my experiences in Kosovo. The Open Society Fund was almost the only party active in building civil society in Kosovo from 1992 to 1999. There was no will whatsoever to step into that area of activity and to try to do something. In fact, I had arguments with high-level officials in the State Department on this very issue. In November 1998, one of them told me that they were not ready to be involved in building civil society in Kosovo because it was very risky. It could mean, he said, strengthening those persons who wanted to separate from Yugoslavia. He called them secessionists.

I asked him whether he thought inaction would yield a result other than secession. I argued that if they didn't support civil society, a terrorist might step in to solve the problems in a different way. It was not difficult to think about such a possibility. Only three days later, the first event in Drenica took place. Only three days later.

My question today is this: Does the administration in the United States, and not only the United States, really believe in the idea of civil society? Do the policymakers believe civil society could be an alternative to ethnic violence, to tyranny, or are these only words? Is this only rhetoric?

In the winter of 1996-97, we had pro-democracy demonstrations in Belgrade and, in fact, in the entire country. They lasted for three months and developed within a powerful pro-democracy movement. I remember that a group of American congressmen came to town. They were asked by the American Embassy not to address the crowd in the streets. They had been told that they could go as private citizens, but they were not allowed to address 100,000 people in the streets of Belgrade, not because this was dangerous but because this was not the politics of the moment. One might think this is an isolated incident, or that some diplomat in Belgrade did not understand what was going on very well. Yet, a few months later in 1997, my colleague John Fox and I asked the leaders of USAID whether they were ready to support the cities in Serbia whose governments had been taken over by the opposition. (These were the same cities, by the way, that played a crucial role in getting rid of Milosevic three years later.) This was before Kosovo and the NATO intervention. The answer we received was that USAID was not planning to help these cities for a few years. They said it was too soon. They were still thinking about it. I don't know what would have happened if the Europeans had not gotten their act together in the year 2000 and had not finally started supporting these cities. Milosevic might still be sitting in Belgrade today.

Things like this make me think that we have a serious responsibility to ask painful questions. We have to try our best to reach out to the American public with these painful questions. Maybe it is naive, but I think this is the right time. After September 11, there is more sensitivity to issues of global relevance. So I believe this is the time to address the issue of prevention.

Prevention costs a lot. But intervention costs even more. I am absolutely convinced that at least certain interventions could have been avoided if there had been more serious preventive action.

One of the issues which bothers me and many of my friends and colleagues in Belgrade and the Balkans nowadays concerns America's decision to pull back from the International Criminal Court. Can there ever be an efficient, permanent international court without the participation of the United States, the only global power? We all know the answer to this question. I am absolutely convinced that only an international criminal court can act as a preventive instrument.

A few days ago I spoke with some people who are quite well informed about the situation in Macedonia in 2001. They are convinced that the existence of the war crimes tribunal in The Hague played an important role in limiting the number of victims in the Macedonia conflict. Both sides knew that they had to restrain themselves; otherwise, they might find themselves in The Hague. But this is only a temporary tribunal. At the very beginning of the Milosevic trial, Washington announced that it should close down in about 2008. This was not a very smart move. It was very discouraging for people who would like to see just such an institution become a preventive mechanism.

The only way I see that we can bring this issue to the forefront of public discussion is to contact our friends in the media. We have to organize public debates. We have to reach out to the American public, because public reaction is an important element for changing policies in Washington.

I am not only critical of inaction and a lack of prevention coming from Washington. I was shocked, for instance, when the former president of France, Giscard D'Estaigne, was appointed to the most important post in the European Union, the head of the intergovernmental summit that will decide how the Union will be enlarged. The same Giscard D'Estaigne besmirched by scandal related to one of the worst dictators Africa had in its recent history.

David Rohde: I'm curious about Bill's thoughts on Nigeria and its government. Have you seen any positive changes or developments?

Bill Berkeley: You probably know more about Nigeria than I do since you've been there more recently. So I tread hesitantly on that territory, because I was last in Nigeria in 1984. But this isn't going to stop me from answering your question.

The military folks ousted from power over the last few years are seeking to regain a footing by mobilizing supporters on ethnic grounds and destabilizing the existing status quo. They are calling for imposition of Sharia law, for example, and making appeals on ethnic grounds and recalling and exploiting existing grievances between Muslims and Christians. I do not know whether this is a significant departure from the pattern I described earlier. In Nigeria, from what I understand, there's a significant corollary. Nigeria was dominated for most of its postcolonial, independent history by the northern Muslim-dominated military. In the elections of 1999, a Yoruba man, a Christian, Olusegun Obasanjo, became president. Wisely, if not always successfully, he instituted anticorruption laws and swept from government a lot of folks who had their snouts in one of the world's most corrupt economies, an economy with abundant resources, oil resources. It is a classic example of a potentially prosperous nation reduced to poverty by corruption and unaccountable government.

My sense is a lot of the old military cronies of Sani Abacha, who ruled Nigeria before Obasanjo, are playing dirty, playing the ethnic card and the religious card. It is worth emphasizing that, in much of Africa, including Nigeria, religion plays a role analogous to the role ethnicity plays in a country like Sudan. In Nigeria, Islam and Christianity are used by political entrepreneurs as a badge of legitimacy, as a means of mobilization, as a means of divide and rule.

Congo and the International Criminal Court

Aryeh Neier: Let me relate Congo to what Sonja was saying about the International Criminal Court. On April 11, ten countries ratified the International Criminal Court, bringing the total number to 66. One of the countries was Congo, which faxed in its ratification and had it accepted by the United Nations. This is an immensely interesting development, because several other African governments have invaded Congo and are exploiting its natural resources. Zimbabwe, for example, is harvesting timber there. And this is the principal revenue Mugabe is now getting internationally. By ratifying the treaty for the International Criminal Court, Congo is putting all of its invaders—Rwanda, Uganda, Angola, Namibia, and Zimbabwe—on notice that if their troops are in Congo after July 1 and if they commit war crimes, they face indictment by the court. Most of the countries that have ratified the agreement have governments with the least to fear from the International Criminal Court. Congo itself can't solve the multiple invasions. So, by ratifying, it's using the International Criminal Court to put pressure on the various invaders. It's an interesting development that I think the proponents of the International Criminal Court hadn't taken into account when they were advocating its creation.

Something similar may take place in Colombia. President Andres Pastrana is trying to secure ratification before he leaves office. This would put pressure on the different factions in Colombia, the right-wing militias and the guerrilla groups, because they too could face indictment before the International Criminal Court. So, in a peculiar way, the court is being used in a few places as a way to try to resolve some of these seemingly intractable conflicts by threatening those participating in them.

Bill Berkeley: Let me make a comment about Congo, a slightly different slant on the same point you're making. My comment relates to the collapse of the effort to send a UN investigation team into Jenin and how this could undermine future UN investigations. In Congo, back in 1996 or 1997, then-President Laurent Kabila blocked a UN investigation. It was widely thought at the time that Kabila blocked the investigation because he feared that investigators would dig up evidence and provide grounds to indict him.

Aryeh Neier: Right. He objected to the Chilean Roberto Garetton as the investigator because he regarded Garetton as a particular threat. Kofi Annan really discredited himself, I think, by bowing to the withdrawal of Roberto Garetton. Garetton ultimately, I think, went back to Congo. The UN managed to right itself. But it was a very bad moment.

Bill Berkeley: Congo is a very important example of the problem with organized crime and organized criminal interests. In eastern Congo there are all sorts of minerals in play, including something called coltan, which is the basis for cell phones—an ironic image, backward eastern Congo providing the basic component for cell phones and other modern equipment. But not just criminal syndicates and criminal actors are on the ground in Congo. There are many legitimate businesses from all over the world involved in looting Congo's banks and trading companies and exporters. A powerful report by a UN investigative commission on the looting of eastern Congo highlighted the role of the governments of Congo, Rwanda, and Uganda. These allies of the United States essentially played the role of mafia godfathers for legitimate businesses from countries as far afield as Malaysia and Indonesia. The European companies included firms from Belgium, Great Britain, and France. A company from Arkansas was one of the first while the Clinton administration was still in power. Mysteriously, as soon as Laurent Kabila seized large amounts of territory in Congo, a company in, I think it was, Hope, Arkansas, got one of the first so-called contracts with Kabila to loot the country's diamonds.

Aryeh Neier: I should mention an issue that arose at a meeting of our African foundations that the Open Society Institute convened in Johannesburg.

One proposal that won a kind of endorsement there is coming up in quite significant ways politically. It has emerged from the London-based organization Global Witness, which has done superb work on the connection between resource exploitation, corruption, and arms trade, on the one hand, and human rights abuses on the other. Global Witness has done much of its work in Africa. It recently published a very good report on Angola calling for public disclosure of the payments resource-exploitation corporations make to governments. It is a fairly simple proposal, but the idea is catching on. The Open Society Institute supports the proposal.

One of the companies that I think has behaved more responsibly than other oil companies in Angola is BP Amoco, a relatively minor player in the country. It did disclose its payments to the Angolan government. As a result, the Angolan government decided to exclude BP Amoco from Angola. Other companies, like ExxonMobil, are refusing to disclose their payments, but Global Witness was able to track down one Caribbean bank account that contained $1.1 billion and had as its signatories two colleagues of President José Eduardo dos Santos.

This is a measure of how much money is paid out in corruption in the resource exploitation of these countries. Public disclosure is a simple requirement. The stock exchanges that list these resource companies might require companies to make these disclosures. National legislation might also be passed in the countries where these companies operate. All by itself, public disclosure would have a significant impact on curbing corruption as well as curbing the conflicts that are, so often, driven by control of resources.

Curbing the Economic Incentives for Conflict

Bill Berkeley: If there are solutions to these conflicts, they must include a change in the economic calculus. The international community must devise ways to curb the economic incentives fueling these wars.

Individual Africans all over the continent are embracing civil society at great risk to themselves and to their livelihoods. A tremendous human rights movement has developed in Africa over the past decade. Institutions of civil society have sprouted up all across the continent. Africans don't need to be told how to solve their problems. The people know how to solve them and are doing what they can to build institutions of civil society as well as institutions of government that are accountable. They need to be supported and embraced. I think this is the best that we can do at this stage in Africa.

Samantha Power: I have a question for Sonja about prevention. It seems that there are many structural reasons that keep prevention from finding a place at the top of the U.S. government's list of things to do. I want to get your reaction to these structural reasons and think about how we can combat them.

One reason stems from the fact that politics is short term by definition. People lack the imagination and the political incentives to think in systemic ways, whether it's an investment in the International Criminal Court or in foreign aid or in education. This is just not how the individual in Washington works.

Second, given that we're all realistic idealists or idealistic realists, we have talked a lot about political pressure. There's an old Fleet Street saying, "If it bleeds, it leads." So if it doesn't bleed, it doesn't lead. Press attention is sparse in places that are in the early stages of conflict, stages in which preventive measures might work. You cannot generate sufficient political pressure in the absence of press attention.

The third problem is this: When you have prevented a conflict, you don't know it, and you don't get any political credit for it. It is hard to identify the causal roots to events, even events welcomed by local citizens or by the international community. Civil society promoters receiving U.S. aid would be, in most cases anyway, reluctant to boast about the connection. Given that it is hard for politicians or policymakers to think in terms of the costs of failing to take preventive measures, are there ways to draw more attention to the benefits in order to increase the political incentives to acting preventively?

Sonja Licht: Well, as you are aware, this is a very difficult question whose answer some of us have spent almost our entire adult lives trying to figure out.

I will describe an experience I had when the Helsinki Citizens' Assembly was created in October 1990 in Prague. I think it was a unique event, at least in our lifetimes. A thousand people from Canada to Azerbaijan—politicians, civic activists, trade unionists, and so on—came together for the first time to try to create a movement to integrate the Helsinki countries from below. A number of different things were achieved at the assembly, but, for various reasons, we did not achieve our main goal.

A friend of mine, a Swede of Hungarian origin, asked his friend from the *New York Times*, whether he was going to report on this event, which was opened, by the way, by Vaclav Havel. The guy from the *Times* said, "Nothing happened, so, unfortunately, I cannot report from this event."

I am afraid that this is always the situation. I would like to see a global movement put real pressure on politicians to become more socially aware. But this is idealism, utopia. If I want to be a realistic idealist, as you said, I would say we must aim at a more realistic target. And this can be done only through the media. I believe that enhancing the sense of social responsibility among the media would have to be our first and foremost task. When Milosevic fell, Ivan Vejvoda and I had interviews with dozens and dozens of journalists. I am always the bad cop. I was the first one to say that enough was enough and that I was not going to talk to anyone anymore about one single topic. All they wanted to figure out was whether Milosevic fell because the opposition and the Otpor People's Movement received foreign assistance. It was a most artificial approach.

Finally, when I lost my patience, and this happens sometimes, I told one of them, "Listen, I can guarantee you that the Kolubara miners never got a single penny of USAID money, European Union money, or, in fact, Soros money. And they brought Milosevic down." The journalist looked at me blankly. I analyzed the situation for him. I tried to describe the influence of Otpor, and small groups, and larger groups, and Radio B92, and others, on the Kolubara miners. You need a little bit of knowledge to follow this. But he did not have that knowledge. You know, many journalists who run in are the ones who are the fastest, and the fastest are not always the smartest. So, the problem is knowledge, because we cannot have a socially responsible media without more knowledgeable people. You need people who really know what they are talking about.

Without a serious, ongoing campaign for preventive action, we will never be able to make politicians believe that action is necessary even though it doesn't bring immediate results. In fact, it sometimes brings results that are exactly the opposite. I really think we have to get out of our offices and our classes and become activists again if we really care about these issues.

Complicity and Impunity
in the Iran-Iraq War

Moderator: *Viola Zentai*, acting director, Center for Policy Studies, CEU,
and project manager, Local Government Initiative, OSI
Speaker: *Joost Hiltermann*
Comments: *Paul Roe*, assistant professor, Department of International
Relations and European Studies, Central European University

Viola Zentai: Joost Hiltermann will explore the human rights abuses and atrocities that took place during and after the Iran-Iraq war.

Joost Hiltermann: I will speak about the Iran-Iraq war and what happened to the Kurds in 1988, make some comments about the role of international actors in genocide, and say something about complicity and impunity as two particularly important concepts in this respect.

At this conference, we're dealing not only with the actual perpetrators of genocide, but also with the accomplices to genocide and the bystanders. These are broad terms that include parties that are not necessarily providing the tools by which genocide is committed. For now, no law criminalizes the acts of accomplices. So I can only make a moral argument. I note, however, that the Rome Statute lays out the role of accessories. Since the International Criminal Court will not act retrospectively, the events that took place in 1988 will not fall under its remit.

In terms of the role of accomplices, I'm making an argument about complicity in genocide. All states have an obligation under the genocide convention to prevent and suppress the act of genocide. My argument is that this is very difficult when major world powers are, first of all, aware of what is going on and, second, assisting the perpetrators of these acts.

Four out of the five permanent members of the Security Council backed Iraq during the Iran-Iraq war. This was during the Cold War when the Soviet Union and the United States were at loggerheads. On this issue, however, they were very much on the same side of the fence. Only China did not back Iraq. It remained neutral. The Security Council showed its support for Iraq repeatedly through resolutions heavily biased in Iraq's favor.

Why did the United States and the others support Iraq? The bottom line in the Gulf is always oil. Access to oil and the need to keep oil affordable were one factor. Another factor was the change of regime in Iran. The Shah of Iran, the United States' guardian in the Gulf, had fallen. He was replaced by a regime that was unpredictable, a regime that took Western hostages and became hated. If we see any kind of sentiment in the Iran-Iraq war, it is that, while the United States and France and Britain and others strongly disliked Iraq, they disliked Iran even more.

UN and U.S. Support for Iraq's Acts of Aggression

The Iran-Iraq war started with the invasion of Iran by Iraq in September 1980. The presence of Iraqi troops on Iranian territory marked the war during its first two years. During that period, the Security Council issued one resolution, meekly calling for an end to the fighting. It did not ask Iraq to withdraw its troops from Iranian territory despite the fact that the invasion and occupation of Iran were acts of aggression. Things changed when the Iranians managed, despite all predictions, to push the Iraqis back out of Iran in May and June of 1982, after almost two years of war. The Iranians then proceeded to enter Iraqi territory. The Security Council quickly passed a resolution calling for the immediate withdrawal of Iranian troops from Iraq. Also, the United States began to tilt toward Iraq, a tilt that would, in money terms, amount to billions of dollars in credit guarantees and other forms of assistance by the time Iraq invaded Kuwait in August 1990. These credits and other forms of assistance were not direct military aid. But allied countries like Jordan and Saudi Arabia were encouraged to provide U.S. weapons and other arms to Iraq. This massive support clearly gave a green light to Iraq.

In my view, both Iraq and Iran committed war crimes on a systematic basis. They both targeted civilians. During the "war of the cities," for example, they launched missiles at each other's urban centers. They both fired upon ships in the Gulf. Iran, in particular, used child soldiers, even in mine-clearing operations. The Western states got away with this green-light policy toward Iraq, despite its atrocities, for two reasons. The first is the "fog-of-war" factor. It is very hard to know what is really happening during warfare, who is doing what to whom. The second is the fact that both Iran and Iraq were hermetically closed societies at the time. Iraq was a totalitarian police state; Iran was under a revolutionary regime that also blocked access to independent outsiders. Except for a few foolhardy and brave individuals who managed to smuggle themselves into these countries, especially into the Kurdish areas, there were no independent observers who were on the ground and able to observe what was going on during this war.

The literature on the Iran-Iraq war is remarkable for its systematic distortion of the facts. There is no single account I can think of that provides an independent, dispassionate, and accurate view of this war. I'm not about to write that account. My focus is much more limited. But if there are any historians out there who are interested, there is a wealth of information that would allow for thorough research on this critical period, the 1980s, and especially on the war and what happened to the two societies during this period.

During the war, a decades-old Kurdish insurgency managed to ratchet up its fight against the Iraqi government because Iraqi troops were mobilized in the south, where the Iranians were attacking most vehemently. The Kurds were able to take over swathes of the countryside in the north. The Kurdish rebel parties received logistical and military support from Iran, essentially becoming a fifth column associated with the Iranian war effort. The Kurds were seen as Iranian proxies, even though they had their own longstanding claims that had nothing to do with Iran.

In response to the Kurd attacks, Iraq stepped up its counter-insurgency campaign. Its preoccupation with the Iranian military assault in the south, however, prevented the Iraqi government from doing much about the Kurdish insurgency until about 1987. What happened during 1987 is critically important. In March of 1987, Saddam Hussein, the Iraqi leader, appointed his cousin Ali Hasan al-Majid to be the governor of the north. The Kurds referred to him as "Ali Chemical," because he began the use of chemical weapons against them. Iraq had already used chemical weapons against the Iranian forces during the war, probably in 1983, but definitely in 1984, which is well documented. The U.S. government protested the use of chemical weapons and even imposed a ban on the sale of chemical precursors to Iraq in 1984. It also made demarches to the government of West Germany, because West German companies were supplying these same materials to Iraq. So the use of chemical weapons was very well documented and very well known.

In 1987, Iraq started using these weapons against its own people. From the beginning, it was targeting not only the Kurdish rebel parties, but also Kurdish civilians. To some extent, the rebels were mixed in with civilians and operating from villages located in the valleys in the higher-elevation areas of the Kurdish-populated section of northern Iraq. The Kurdish region is divided between high northern mountains and flatlands toward the Arab-populated region in the south. All the Kurdish mountain villages are in valleys, but some valleys are higher than others. One of the first things Ali Chemical did was order chemical attacks. Second, he ordered the destruction of all Kurdish villages in the lower valleys that were accessible to Iraqi troops at the time. The troops destroyed these villages, forcibly removing their inhabitants and placing them in resettlement camps. The third measure Ali Chemical undertook was to issue, in June of 1987, a couple of orders that are smoking-gun documents, as far as we are concerned. These orders declared large areas of the Kurdish-populated territory to be prohibited, free-fire zones. Anyone seen in the prohibited zones was liable to be shot on sight. The prohibited zones consisted of the entire Kurdish region less the towns and the roads connecting the towns. These zones included the areas where the Iraqi troops had destroyed the villages. But they also included the higher valleys, where the Iraqi troops had not reached. In these higher valleys there were still thriving Kurdish villages. So civilians living in these villages from that time onward, could be shot on sight.

The two military orders from June 1987 were a blueprint for the military campaign that started in February 1988, after the winter snows had melted. By this time, Iraq also had a fairly clear sense that the war with Iran was winding down. Iran had finally accepted a Security Council resolution laying out a plan to end the war. Iraq had become much stronger militarily thanks to Western assistance. Now it could comfortably redeploy some of its troops to the north.

Chemical Weapons Destroy Kurdish Resistance

The first action Iraq undertook, in what became known as the Anfal campaign, was to attack the headquarters of one of the two major Kurdish parties, the Patriotic Union of Kurdistan, the PUK. The Iraqi army attacked the headquarters on a daily basis with chemical weapons and rocket and air attacks for about three weeks. But the headquarters were well ensconced in a very high valley. The local villagers and guerrillas had moved into caves so they weren't really affected by either the chemicals or the shells. The Iraqi pressure was so strong, however, that the Kurdish leaders decided that they needed to launch another military action. They decided to take a Kurdish town from the Iraqis in order to force the Iraqi troops to pull back from their headquarters. The Kurds launched their attack on March 15, 1988, the first time that a major Kurdish town had been taken by the Kurds themselves. In turn, Iraq, seeing this as a brazen act, decided to launch a massive retaliation. What happened the next day in Halabja was the first and, still is, history's only major chemical weapons attack on an urban population center. This event went largely unreported until later, when people became interested in it for political reasons. Halabja, which is often referred to in the press as a village, is actually a major town.

What happened in Halabja is an atrocity of major proportions. In fact, if you look at the number of casualties and the singularity of the attack, it is comparable to what happened at the World Trade Center. The population of the World Trade Center was about 80,000; the population of Halabja and its surrounding areas, which were all targeted, was also about 80,000 at the time. The number of casualties in Halabja is estimated at 5,000 to 6,000, which, I remind you, was also the initial estimate at the World Trade Center, though the September 11 death toll has since been revised to just about 3,000. I wouldn't be surprised if the total fatalities at Halabja are actually lower than what has been reported, because nobody has actually done an accurate accounting of it.

The importance of the Halabja attack cannot be underestimated. It demoralized the Kurds and the Kurdish guerrillas and led to their instant defeat. The PUK headquarters, which had resisted concerted Iraqi attacks for weeks, fell within two or three days. The guerrillas withdrew to Iran. The Halabja attack also had a demonstration effect throughout the Kurdish areas. Chemical weapons, although highly lethal in the Halabja case, are not generally a very effective weapon of war. The chemicals are highly volatile, scattering in high winds and often blowing back onto friendly forces. So it is very dangerous for the soldiers in the front lines. There were many cases of friendly fire injuries or deaths on the Iraqi side thanks to Iraq's use of chemical weapons. These cases were later portrayed as Iranian attacks. Many times, Iraqi soldiers didn't realize what was hitting them. Chemical weapons are really weapons of terror.

The Anfal campaign had seven stages after Halabja. On the first day of each stage, the Iraqi forces would use chemical weapons on a couple of villages in the area they were targeting. The effect was amazing. People who had been under artillery shelling and air attacks for years literally packed up whatever they could carry, whether they were near the chemical attack or far away from it, and ran. Some tried to reach a border. In many instances, before they could reach a border, they had to cross a main paved road. On these roads, Iraqi troops were waiting for them. The Iraqi troops gathered up the men, women, and children, tractors, belongings, everything, and took them to transit centers. The tractors stayed in these centers, but the people were trucked to a larger transit center. Here people were sorted by gender essentially and by age, not necessarily by political affiliation. All the men were taken in one group, except for the very old and the very young. The very old men and women were taken in a second group. And the younger women and children were taken in a third group. We have extremely good documentation on everything that happened until this stage because Iraqi secret police documents have become available.

What happened after this is less clear to us, simply because we have no Iraqi documents that describe it. What we know, we know from eyewitnesses, from people who were taken from this transit center to execution sites and managed to escape in miraculous ways. The vast majority of the men went to execution sites far from the Kurdish areas. Bulldozers and armed people were waiting. The victims were gunned down and buried in mass graves. Large numbers of the women and children were similarly taken and systematically murdered at the gravesites and buried under the sands. Only the old men and women were sent to a prison in the southern desert. The conditions were horrible, and many died. The survivors were subsequently released in a general amnesty for Kurds in September 1988, about six months after the beginning of the campaign.

Based upon extensive research in the area, we know that about 100,000 people never returned. The vast majority of these people, if not all of them, were killed at the time or shortly afterwards. After the 1991 Gulf War, there were uprisings in the north and the south of Iraq. In the south, the Iraqi authorities crushed the rebels. In the north, thanks to Western intervention, the Kurds were able to start rebuilding their villages. But, from this moment on, the Kurds were important to the Untied States and other Western powers only to the extent that they kept Saddam Hussein off-balance. This meant that there was actually no development permitted in these areas. No serious infrastructure was built. No industry of any sort could be built. The Kurdish area in northern Iraq has basically been kept as a dependency of Turkey, the United States, and others.

No Accountability for Kurdish Genocide

The United States has obtained large amounts of evidence about what happened to the Kurds but it has refused to do anything with the evidence. We at Human Rights Watch tried to bring a genocide case against Iraq, and tried to obtain American political support. But these efforts came to nought. We also tried to find states that were willing to take up this case, but this too came to nought. Nothing happened despite the fact that the United States, of course, had flip-flopped in its view of Iraq after Iraq had invaded Kuwait.

The case of the Kurds is a case of genocide. It involved 100,000 people, a small genocide in some ways if you compare it to Rwanda or to the Holocaust, but it was systematic, centrally organized and orchestrated. The documents make this very clear.

So what are the implications of this? Here we move from the issue of complicity to the issue of impunity. First, there were all kinds of regional reverberations. The continuing demonstration effect of Halabja became evident in 1991, when the Kurds rose up. The moment the Iraqi troops came back to the area, there was a massive flight of Kurds. The chemical attacks on Halabja and other places are the only way to explain the instant panic in 1991. If you ask Kurds, they say they thought they would be attacked with chemical weapons again. It did not matter that no chemicals were used at the time. This demonstration effect still exists today. If an Iraqi incursion were to happen, people would flee in an instant. The second implication of the Kurdish genocide is that it gave Iraq's leaders the confidence that it could get away with mass murder and this may have led them to believe they could get away with the invasion of Kuwait. After all, Iraq may have thought that it could be just as strong a protector of oil as Kuwait had been. Iraq also thought it had legitimate reasons to take Kuwait, mostly financial. So Iraq may have thought that it could get away with taking Kuwait and convincing the United States that it could also keep the price of oil down. This may be, or it may not be. But it deserves further exploration.

A third clear implication of the Kurdish genocide is that Iran, as a direct consequence of Iraq's use of chemical weapons, launched its own programs to develop weapons of mass destruction—chemical weapons, biological weapons, nuclear weapons. There are some stories that Iran used chemical weapons during the Iran-Iraq war, but I have not found a shred of evidence to support this. What is clear is that the Iranians vocally opposed the use of chemical weapons until late in the war. Then they began to say that they might have to use them as the only way to resist the Iraqi chemical weapons attacks. My supposition is that they started developing chemical weapons late in the war; they were ready to use them, but they never did. Iran, by the way, was one of the first countries to ratify the chemical weapons convention that came into being after the Iran-Iraq war. Still, it is suspected of having secret facilities, but I've no way of knowing whether these rumors have any basis in fact.

Another implication of the Kurdish genocide is that when forces from the United States and its allies went into Saudi Arabia, Kuwait, and Iraq in 1991, they had to be prepared for chemical attacks. Israel also feared chemical attacks and had to prepare for their possibility. Everybody obtained gas masks to prepare for the eventuality that Iraq would, yet again, use chemical weapons. These are serious matters. They instill great fear.

But what did the United States gain after all of this? To me, it's unclear. The argument is that, if the United States had not supported Iraq during the Iran-Iraq war, or if the United States had been more even-handed or had tried to end the war, the Iranian revolution would have spread. The Iranian revolution, in turn, might have brought the downfall of some of the key Gulf states, the small Gulf states. Some of them have majority Shiite populations, and Iran is, of course, majority Shiite. So there might have been a domino effect that would have presented a grave threat to Western access to oil.

In the end, of course, it was Iraq that posed the greatest threat to oil, not Iran. But it could have been the other way around, too. It's a very difficult argument. I understand from scholars who've worked in the Gulf states in the 1970s and 1980s that the perceived threats to domestic tranquillity in these states was highly exaggerated. These scholars say the Shiites in the Gulf states, first of all, did not agree with the Iranian revolution. They say there was dissonance in these Gulf states because these states were not democratic.

Just to finish up, Iraq clearly had a protector in the 1980s. But there was a deafening silence when noise, in my view, could have made a difference. The United States was fully aware of Iraqi actions during the Iran-Iraq war. In fact, it was providing the Iraqis with satellite photographs of Iranian troop formations and movements. It had Defense Intelligence Agency people on the ground, including the front lines on the Iraqi side. American diplomats were able to travel, with some difficulty in some cases, and with some courage, through the Kurdish countryside. They reported back about the massive destruction of villages as early as 1987. The only thing that I am not sure the United States knew was the actual fate of the people who were taken during the Anfal campaign in 1988. Even some Kurds—people who were not taken away—thought they went to resettlement camps in the south, because this is what happened after the Iraqis crushed a Kurdish insurgency in 1975.

In my view, the Kurdish genocide could have been prevented. United States support of Iraq might have been a whole lot less wholehearted if there had been domestic opposition. The prerequisite for domestic opposition is information, and at that point the information was not available. What was available was not believed. More seriously, information was distorted or twisted in order to diffuse responsibility. Some reports, for example, said that Iran, as well as Iraq, used chemical weapons.

The argument I'm trying to develop in my book is that the genocide could have been averted had there been early intervention. This intervention would have been possible on the basis of information that was clearly available to the government and, to some extent, the international public.

The Academic's Role:
Providing a Framework for Ethnic Conflicts

Viola Zentai: Paul Roe will talk about the role of academia in providing a framework for explaining ethnic conflicts.

Paul Roe: I find myself in a slightly odd position. I have never lived in a country or a region that has been afflicted by conflict. I have not reported from any country about conflicts that have taken place. And I have not been engaged in any extensive empirical research about a particular case of ethnic conflict or, in the context of Iraq and Iraq, a more traditional case of inter-state war. What I have been involved in is looking more conceptually and thematically at different approaches to the question of ethnic violence and conflict.

So what I hope to do is to provide some bones for the very rich flesh that we've had in the talks by our panelists. This can help us make sense of what the other panelists have said by locating it in a broader framework. I hope to raise some questions about the bigger questions of responsibility and intervention.

My discipline of international relations, in its traditional incarnation, has been extremely bad at addressing the question of ethnic conflict. The traditional approach for analyzing ethnic conflicts borrows from Kenneth Waltz's classic three-level approach to the phenomenon of generic warfare—the levels of human nature, states, or the international system. When we apply this three-level approach to the study of warfare within a state, what we have is a notion that human nature tends to translate itself into some kind of mass hostility. The masses react spontaneously to various provocations, and it all spills over.

Now what tends to be conflated in this bottom-up approach is the notion that primordial ethnic hatreds are driving this type of conflict. On the level of human nature, there is the idea that emotion naturally spills out of people who have been harboring grievances over the centuries, providing the dynamic force for such conflicts.

The second level instructs us to locate causes at the level of the states. It also tells us that within the international system there is a dichotomy between so-called good states and bad states. Applying this to the intra-state level, what we find is a top-down picture. This has generally tended to translate into an examination of the role of governments, political elites, and leaderships in whatever form they may take. I think this corresponds closely to Bill Berkeley's approach, which is to outline how the political elites are driving ethnic conflicts for their own selfish interests.

The third level deals with structural considerations. This has been the most problematic area, because, in the inter-state sphere, structural considerations equate to the notion of an anarchical international system that generates self-help behavior. And at the intra-state level there has been some notion of how to translate this by recreating a picture of how we might have anarchical conditions within the state that may generate self-help conditions.

This three-level typology has some rather interesting things to say both about the notion of responsibility and questions pertaining to intervention. If we locate responsibility on the bottom level of mass hostility, primordialism, ancient hatreds, then we tend to reach the conclusion that it is difficult to assign responsibility. Who would be responsible? When we're dealing with a spontaneous outburst of hatreds that people have been harboring for generations, it is difficult to pin responsibility on particular individuals or structures that we can hold accountable. It is a messy picture, a Hobbesian war of all against all. And it is more than difficult to intervene in such a context, because intervention means imposing some kind of solution. Decision-makers have tended to conclude that, if ancient hatreds are driving the conflict, then the conflict is going to carry on regardless. Nothing can be done about it. They say, "Let's just let them fight it out, and sort it out for themselves, because there's not much that we can do to impose a long-lasting settlement."

At the second level, we have a notion that is often called "conflict entrepreneurship," where self-interested elites provoke conflict to stay in power. In this case, responsibility is quite easy to attribute. We pinpoint particular leaders and organizational structures and say, "Yes, these people are responsible for whipping up the hatred in a very instrumental way and mobilizing masses, or sections of the masses, toward violence." In this situation, we probably have a clearer picture of how we should intervene. There are perpetrators and there are victims. An intervention would be designed to take action against these identifiable perpetrators. So, in a way, we can provide ourselves with a clear picture of how we can take sides in the conflict in a way that the bottom-up approach doesn't give us.

The third level is kind of interesting in itself. It involves the notion of structure. On this level, again, it is very hard to attribute responsibility. One of the concepts that we're dealing with here involves the role of the security dilemma in ethnic conflicts. The security dilemma tends to give the impression that the self-help dynamics at the intra-state level have a momentum of their own. The actors or perpetrators involved in the conflict tend to become trapped by these structural imperatives. The situation somehow manifests itself as something not of their own making. They are compelled to do certain things. There are unintended consequences in the end. So, in a way, responsibility is very difficult to locate. It tends to diffuse the causes of the conflict away from particular individuals or groups.

The Security Dilemma and Ethnic Cleansing

The security dilemma raises interesting problems regarding intervention. Chaim Kaufmann, associate professor at Lehigh University, has a rather controversial approach. If we want to solve conflicts that are driven by the security dilemma, he advocates endorsing or aiding ethnic cleansing in a way. So, in a rather demographically mixed area such as Bosnia, where groups are not cohesive enough to defend themselves against possible attack, what we do is create bigger, more cohesive, more defensible units. What we do is get ourselves involved in aiding population transfer and creating mini-states. This is what we seem to have come to in Bosnia.

I think there is another notion of responsibility contained within all these three approaches. It is the responsibility of the academic. The academic is responsible for producing the tools, the lenses through which we actually look at conflicts. These conceptual tools bring with them certain implications about actor responsibility and about strategies of intervention or nonintervention. Given this, the academic has to be very careful in attributing how particular concepts have played roles in particular conflicts. For instance, the security dilemma has been extensively used, particularly in the case of former Yugoslavia. Bound up with this notion of structural imperatives and self-help is the notion that it is difficult to attribute actor responsibility. Somehow actors can excuse themselves by saying, "We were compelled to do certain things. The structure of the situation forced us to do that. We were simply trying to ensure our own security in the anarchical situation we encountered." This has potentially serious repercussions. And we, as academics, have to be very careful about them. We can't stand behind this veil of neutrality, because we are the ones providing the conceptual tools, the lenses, through which people will interpret these conflicts.

From here I want to pull out a few of the things from Joost's work and relate this all back to how the study of international relations and security studies has approached the question of ethnic conflict.

Joost brings out an extremely important point. There were certain consequences of the Iran-Iraq war that were a manifestation of the international community and the United States failing to address human rights violations and, in particular, the Iraqi use of chemical weapons. One of Joost's conclusions asks how we are to incorporate this notion of human and minority rights within the strategic consideration of states. What is implicit in Joost's conclusion is that, at a minimum, states must realize that unless they deal with human rights violations, these violations have the potential to have a knock-on effect. One violation will affect something else, and it will in turn affect something else and create a situation that is even worse, even more acute. And it will be in the national interest to deal with this resulting situation.

So, in some ways, we should have greater foresight in anticipating how human rights violations have consequences for national and international security. I wholeheartedly agree with what Joost is saying, and I think the big problem for security studies is to address the question of how to incorporate approaches to human and minority rights into the field. It is a question of trying to reevaluate what is the national interest so that human and minority rights have a part in it.

I think there is also a bigger problem. And this problem is that we've come to define security as a wholly negative concept. If you take a classic definition of security, you tend to find something like "the pursuit of freedom from threat." So the starting point for security studies is that we have an identifiable threat that we should take action against. We should look to eradicate the source of this threat, of this insecurity. This is a wholly negative conception inasmuch as what security studies does not address is what came before the threat. It requires answering why a threat ever arose in the first place.

Some scholars in the discipline are trying to answer this question by, very logically, introducing a notion of positive security. What positive security is, however, isn't so clear. But certainly positive security is predicated upon preventing something that could possibly happen.

I will put this in a slightly different context. Salman Rushdie made a very incisive point commenting on the post–September 11 situation. He said that we, particularly in the West, in the United States and elsewhere, are extremely good at saying what we're against but not very good about saying what we're for. Now, I would like to link this back to our discussion about "Different Notions of Responsibility." As far as I remember, our conversation was very good at doing what Rushdie is warning us about. We were saying, "Well, we can document a whole number of cases where we didn't intervene. And perhaps we should have intervened. And this is bad. And we're against not intervening." But we didn't clearly formulate a notion of "why on earth should we be bothered with getting involved in other people's wars." It is very easy to say that we should intervene or that it's been obviously a catastrophic failure that we haven't. We speak about things in a negative way, and we're not very good at saying what the positive is or defining exactly what it is that we're for.

How can we build this positive notion of security? How can we get this kind of approach into the discipline? It's a hell of a question in a way, and nobody's been very good at fleshing out what this is. But academia has a responsibility to do it. The English philosopher Michael Oakeshott, talking about teaching politics in a university, said that the great thing about the academic is that he or she has the luxury of being able to think about things in a way that is not constrained by the practicalities, by things that go on out there in the world. We are not constrained by the notion that "Well, you know what decision-makers are like. They're never going to go for this, are they." Oakeshott was saying, "The academic has a responsibility to come up with new ways of thinking that will have some kind of filter-down effect."

I'm as lost as most people are about how we address these issues. But I hope there is some way of stimulating this conversation so we can address the positive, so we can break out of this framework of wholly negative terms, so we can have some impact somewhere down the line on decision-making.

Coming to Terms: Tribunals, Truth Commissions, and International Law

Moderator: *Gara LaMarche*, vice president, Open Society Institute, and director of OSI's U.S. Programs
Speaker: *Dinah PoKempner*
Comments: *Iván Székely*, counselor, Open Society Archives

Gara LaMarche: We're concluding this conference with discussions of issues surrounding tribunals, truth commissions, and international law. The first session will deal with the failure of the tribunal for the Khmer Rouge in Cambodia, about which Dinah PoKempner is going to speak. Then Iván Székely, of the Open Society Archives, former chief counselor of the Parliamentary Commissioner for Data Protection and Freedom of Information, will comment.

Dinah PoKempner: I'm going to try to be a little bit more upbeat, or, at least, leave us thinking in more positive ways. But I may not succeed. Since so many people have presented case studies, I'm going to try to present my topic using a case study to give you some context for comparing and contrasting. I will start with a brief synopsis of what happened in Cambodia.

The lead-up to the Khmer Rouge revolution in Cambodia was the ouster of King Sihanouk. He had been Cambodia's political leader for years and a successful leader in the nonaligned movement, much to the irritation of the United States. He was replaced by Lon Nol, a thoroughly corrupt and ineffectual general, who acquiesced to the United States incursion into Cambodia in pursuit of the Viet Cong. The incursion threw Cambodia into the war, and the country suffered great loss of life and disruption of the economy. Sihanouk called on young patriotic Cambodians to join him in forming a resistance force.

The resistance at that point was primarily the Khmer Rouge. The Khmer Rouge movement began with a circle of young Cambodian intellectuals in Paris. It was nurtured and financed by Russia and the Vietnamese in an effort to create an Indo-Chinese federation of communist movements. Ultimately, however, China was the principal sponsor of the people who would emerge as the leaders of the Khmer Rouge movement. They took on a Maoist ideology. By the time they led a swift revolution, a successful take-over of the country in April of 1975, they saw their task as the complete reconstruction of Cambodian society. The reconstruction began with a somewhat predictable purge of all persons associated with the former government, the republican government. The purge quickly spread into massacres of ethnic Vietnamese. Then it evolved into internal party purges, which accelerated as the fear that Vietnam, acting through the section of the party more closely allied with it, was trying to overturn the revolution.

Vietnam responded to what were increasing attacks by Cambodia on Vietnamese villages and incursions onto Vietnamese soil. It again invaded Cambodia swiftly and successfully in January of 1979, installing a new government of Khmer Rouge defectors. By that time, we think, two million people had been killed—between one-fifth and one-fourth of Cambodia's entire population.

Death from Starvation, Disease, and Wearing Eyeglasses

Most of these people died of starvation and disease. Their deaths were the result of the Khmer Rouge's truly insane agricultural and social policies. The Khmer Rouge's goal was to make Cambodia develop faster than any communist country had ever developed and to exceed the prosperity of the ancient kingdom of Cambodia within the space of several years. To this end, they embarked on fantastical projects such as a new national irrigation system that would have required water to flow uphill. The result was an economic and agricultural disaster. Starvation and disease as well as systemic purges and murders resulted in a tremendous loss of life. The Khmer Rouge eradicated the entire infrastructure of Buddhism and most of the educated class. People who wore eyeglasses, for example, were considered politically suspect and summarily executed. So, by 1979, Cambodia wound up with almost no one who could be called a professional.

I went to Cambodia first during the Paris Accords. At that time, people were estimating that there were seven professionally trained lawyers in the entire country. It is very difficult in Cambodia to find people who remember the society of the 1960s. Too many people died, and those who escaped have never wanted to go back. This is a level of social destruction that I think is unique.

The other thing that distinguishes Cambodia from some of the other cases mentioned at this conference is the role of the international community. Although the Khmer Rouge were an indigenous revolutionary movement, Cambodians do assign the international community a heavy role. Cambodians do not ask, "Why didn't you save us from the Khmer Rouge?" Rather, they ask, "Why did you isolate us once the Khmer Rouge were driven out? Why did you recognize them and give Cambodia a seat at the UN? Why did you starve and isolate our successor government?"

There are questions about the role of the U.S. bombing, the roles of France, China, Vietnam, and all the contributors to the conditions that made the Khmer Rouge rise to power possible. But the Khmer Rouge committed actual atrocities during a time when they had completely sealed the country from outside influences. There is some truth to the idea that people outside didn't know what was going on until very late in the game, until after most people had died.

So, that's the context. Now to the tribunal issue.

Before I talk about why the tribunal failed, however, I'd just like to read you this snippet from the *Phnom Penh Post*. It appeared in January of 2002. It is the reply of a survivor named Chum Mey, to the question, "Why would you like to see a trial?" Chum Mey, a blue-collar mechanic, was one of the many people who were sent to the torture center of Choeung Ek in Phnom Penh and brutally tortured. (People were usually tortured until they had given the appropriate confession linking them to involvement with the CIA and Hanoi and whatever other paranoid confessions the Khmer Rouge demanded to hear.)

Chum Mey survived—one of a small number that did—because he knew how to fix sewing machines when the Khmer Rouge needed someone to fix sewing machines. He said he hoped the Khmer Rouge would go on trial: "I'm waiting for it. Every day my soul is wandering and sometimes I think the Khmer Rouge still remain. If a trial were held, my feelings about that time would improve. I still do not know who was wrong and who was right. I don't know why the Khmer Rouge killed people or why they wanted to eliminate their own Khmer race. As a victim . . . I want to know why the UN recognized the Khmer Rouge and why it wants a trial now. A trial would give relief to the families of the victims. Many people have told me their loved ones were killed in [the torture center]. They also want to see the trial. Without a trial, their souls will keep wandering."

I found this comment poignant. The idea of wandering souls captures the moral confusion Cambodia is experiencing now, 20 years after the fact with nothing put to rest. There are many other things I want to pick apart in this description, so I'll just leave these words in your minds for a moment and come back.

On February 8, 2002, the United Nations announced it was withdrawing from negotiations with the Cambodian government about the tribunal. The reason given was that the Cambodian government had pre-empted negotiations with the UN by passing a domestic law establishing a tribunal and then refusing to give the United Nations a memorandum of understanding that would take legal precedence over that domestic law. This was seen as Prime Minister Hun Sen's way of end-running the UN and getting the provisions he wanted.

The withdrawal of the UN was long anticipated by those in contact with the UN Secretariat. Many people in Cambodia, however, were left in a complete state of shock. The announcements caused an immediate outcry, most of it condemning the UN for withdrawing. There were a lot of views as to why the UN had let the people of Cambodia down once again. The very few people who supported this decision came from the international human rights community or, surprisingly, the Cambodian human rights community. Their position put them in an immediate dilemma, because it is very odd for human rights people to be seen opposing a law creating a tribunal.

Among the reasons articulated by the UN for its withdrawal, the issue of amnesty came back again and again as the deal breaker—particularly with reference to the amnesty granted Ieng Sary, the highest-ranking surviving Khmer Rouge leader, for a 1979 conviction of genocide. I think this is a bit of a red herring, and I'll tell you why. Under the Cambodian constitution, the king has the power to grant a pardon, and the government has the power to request the king to grant a pardon. However, the king, a strong supporter of an international tribunal, has no intention of pardoning those the tribunal convicts, and the government has made explicit assurances it will not request pardons. It's debatable that a UN tribunal would have upheld even the concept of amnesty. But even if it did, the crimes of the Khmer Rouge do not fit comfortably into the category of genocide, and there is no bar to pursuing the most likely defendants for crimes against humanity. In fact, the crimes in Cambodia need someone to give them a proper name, someone like Raphael Lemkin, who invented the word "genocide" to describe the Nazis' attempts to exterminate the Jews. The Cambodian people like to call these crimes genocide because the destruction of millions felt like the eradication of the race. And yet, the motivations and the reasons that people were targeted, for the most part, had nothing to do with their ethnicity, with the exception of the Vietnamese and Cham minorities. A genocide argument might fit for these two categories, but that doesn't capture the bulk of the two million.

Moreover, an explicit provision against amnesty would be in direct violation of the Cambodian constitution. You would have had to engage in constitutional reform before you actually created the tribunal. The assurances that the Cambodian government had given that it had absolutely no intentions of asking for an amnesty were still met with some skepticism, given its basic ambivalence about prosecuting Khmer Rouge once it had ended the civil war by pardoning so many of them. Behind the scenes, too, the United States had lost interest in pushing for a tribunal. Despite the statements of Pierre Prosper, U.S. ambassador at large for war crimes, that the United States favors national jurisdictions dealing with these horrific crimes, I don't sense that many in the U.S. administration believed Cambodia's crimes were of strategic importance anymore. There had been a handful of personalities driving the United States policy as it pressured the UN to create a tribunal; but most of these personalities had left by January, or were not highly enough placed anymore to make a difference.

UN Abandonment of the Tribunal: A Fear of Humiliation

Another key factor was that the United Nations became, I think, increasingly convinced that it had gotten itself into a process that could be deeply humiliating. It had accepted a U.S.-brokered concession. Unlike the Sierra Leone and East Timor tribunals, it would allow a majority of judges to be appointed by the Cambodian government and a minority to be nominated by the secretary-general, albeit with a super-majority voting mechanism. This was, if you examined it closely, going to be a very difficult guarantee of integrity to implement. One had to assume that all foreign judges would vote as a block if the Cambodian judges, under pressure from the government, voted together in ways that undermined justice. It would take only one foreign judge voting with the Cambodian civil servants, then, to dismantle the super-majority check, and in that case, the only resort left would be public denunciation or resignation by one of the foreign judges. It required a kind of wild optimism to believe that brave and honest UN-appointed judges would stand up and publicly denounce the tribunal and resign if the Cambodian government tried to manipulate the trial process, as it has tried to manipulate every other trial process in Cambodia. Eventually, people in the Secretariat in New York began to lose faith that they could pull it off. So they got themselves into a situation where it looked as if they were pulling out for publicly articulated reasons that were not that compelling. This put the human rights community in a very difficult position, particularly the Cambodian human rights community. What are they going to do now?

Hun Sen, in characteristic style, has said, "I'm going to give the UN three months to come around, and if they don't come around then we'll go ahead on our own." The UN's not doing anything. And no one's asking it to do anything. So basically everyone in Cambodia is waiting for three months to pass, and then they're going to see what happens.[1]

---

[1] In December 2002, the General Assembly approved a resolution requesting the secretary-general to resume negotiations with Cambodia over the establishment of an Extraordinary Chambers to try the Khmer Rouge. The UN move was supported by key states such as the United States, France, and Japan, but was criticized for recognizing the controversial domestic law passed by Cambodia, establishing a mixed tribunal as a foundation for future negotiations.

If Hun Sen created a Cambodian tribunal, or a Cambodian tribunal that invites pliable international judges, how will the Cambodian human rights community react? A couple years ago, the largest human rights groups in Cambodia collected 80,000 signatures supporting a completely international tribunal. When I've gone to Cambodia and done interviews, I haven't yet met anyone outside Hun Sen's party who believes that a Cambodian tribunal of the Khmer Rouge will be fair or meaningful. That's really quite extraordinary actually. From where do they get this faith in the UN as a guarantor? They have it because of the UN-sponsored elections. People came out in record numbers to vote, despite enormous political violence, because they really believed that if the UN were in control, the election would be fair. So, the key to faith in the tribunal is the idea that the UN would somehow be in control. What's going to happen if there's a compromised tribunal? How should Cambodian activists and intellectuals approach it? What will they do? Will they condemn it? Will they try to make it better? What's going to be their posture? They are all worried about this.

When you ask Cambodians why they want a tribunal, you get answers pretty much like the one from Chum Mey. What you hear a lot is, "I want to know why they did it." This is a very hard statement to understand, because it means a lot of things and I don't think I even understand everything it means. It doesn't mean, for example, "I want to know who killed whom," because this is to some degree known. When you probe, the statement is closer to meaning "I want to have the experience of seeing people called in front of an authority and compelled to answer questions" or "I want the experience of seeing authority called to account." This can be accomplished in a variety of ways other than trials. Some people have said, "I'd be happy if they had to confess before King Sihanouk in the public football stadium." Cambodians also want to know why the Khmer Rouge killed Khmer, because everyone feels it's perfectly understandable why they killed Vietnamese. Cambodians historically despise Vietnamese. It is one of the great ironies that Vietnam rescued the Cambodians, thereby earning only further enmity.

This goes to part of the hollowness at the core of modern Cambodian identity. The Cambodian identity is constructed around the idea of threat and loss, the very old idea that "our neighbors are voracious, taking our land, and intending to annihilate us." They are particularly wary of the Vietnamese, with whom the cultural divide is most stark and who, in modern history, have taken the most land from Cambodia. This idea includes resurrecting the imperium of Angkor, which existed in the 15th and 16th centuries when Cambodia, at the height of its power, dominated the whole region. The loss of Angkor has fed the sense that "we have become such a small unimportant nation that's about to be eaten by its neighbors." There isn't much else, because the Khmer Rouge years swept away much of what else there was.

Buddhism has been highly discredited. There are few educated people. Ordinary teachers are not held in high regard, because they require their students to pay. Government officials are considered former Khmer Rouge. There is a state of impunity in Cambodia that is profound. It is as if almost no one notices it anymore. The government is completely dysfunctional. One joke, truism if you will, has it that four people keep Cambodia running, and if you want to have a bridge in a village, you really have to get the request to Hun Sen, because nobody lower down will take responsibility for anything.

There is also impunity in the more classic sense of nonpunishment. There are so many examples that it's boring to recount them all. Officials do things like shoot a neighbor because the neighbor's dog barks too much. Then nothing happens. Hun Sen's wife organized an attack on Hun Sen's mistress; nothing happened. It's to the point where the human rights groups have documented literally hundreds of instances of serious impunity, of officials killing people within a period spanning less than two years, without consequences. This illuminates why a judicial tribunal is very much desired by Cambodians as a statement against impunity and a particularly appropriate way of dealing with the Khmer Rouge.

King Sihanouk, America's bombing, and the Vietnamese

Other nuances of that basic question "why?" have to do with the ambivalent relation of the Cambodians to the international community. These "whys" have to do with things like the roles of King Sihanouk, America's bombing, and the Vietnamese.

There are many theories about the Vietnamese prevalent among educated people in Phnom Penh. For example, people say that Pol Pot was actually a puppet of the Vietnamese, who turned him to the genocidal purpose of killing the Khmer people. It is an odd idea, but it fits very neatly into popular Cambodian paranoia about the Vietnamese. Now, you might think that this has been written about. And it has been written about. But only by foreigners. One of the other things about Cambodia is that there are almost no modern Cambodian histories written in Khmer. There are almost no survivor accounts in Khmer. Almost everything that has been written about the Khmer Rouge era has been written by the Cambodian diaspora or by foreigners and very little of it has been translated into Khmer. It is only now starting to be translated. There is a documentation center in Cambodia that was set up originally with U.S. State Department money. Its task was to accumulate factual material that would be helpful to the work of a tribunal. And it has tried to translate some of these outsider histories and to do oral history and documentation. It very successfully reestimated the number of deaths at two million by documenting gravesites.

Almost none of this, however, filters down to ordinary Cambodian people. Even this center's very useful publication, a small magazine discussing the Khmer Rouge and the center's activities, is priced at about two dollars, which is more than almost any Cambodian can afford. So, there is little popular dissemination of knowledge. The result is a widespread disbelief among most young Cambodians that things could possibly have been that horrible. I have spoken over and over again with older Cambodians who tell me that their children think that they're just going on for effect when they talk about what they lived through during those years. These children now make up more than half of Cambodia's population.

The perpetrators, the top leaders of the Khmer Rouge, are old and in terrible health and they're going to die, predictably, within the next seven to ten years. So this gives you a sense of a country that is having a memory crisis.

On top of this, one of the conditions laid down for Khmer Rouge who want to defect has been that they don't talk to the press or anyone else about the Khmer Rouge years. One Cambodian man, an intellectual and advisor to the interior ministry who later went into a research institute, took a government-sponsored tour of South Africa to investigate the truth and reconciliation commission there. After returning to Cambodia he wanted to hold a workshop about his findings and impressions, but the government refused permission. You get the sense that a blanket of silence has been thrown over the whole issue.

What can be done? I think truth and reconciliation processes are going to have a lot of the same problems that the tribunal had. There's not that much international interest in cooperating by, for example, opening files. Ironically, all these "why" questions are unlikely to be answered by a trial limited to acts committed between 1975 and 1979. A trial probably would not have gotten into much detail about the international context, because it wasn't that relevant to the actual commission of the crimes. The foreign governments don't want to open their archives and show how their hands were dirty. And there is very little interest on the part of the Cambodian government in bringing up the wider issues of responsibility and possibly spoiling the quiet that amnesties have brought, even though there's virtually no prospect that the country would return to civil war.

So how do we help Cambodia prepare for a moment when accountability is more possible and some memory can be preserved? I tend to think that what's needed right now are initiatives that don't depend on the government's cooperation and endorsement. Cambodia does have a relatively open civil society and a lively press. It needs people to do oral histories, to be trained in writing history. It needs popular dissemination of information. It needs psychological services, so that it is possible to talk about the effects of these years, so that it is possible to leave some trail, some memory.

Cambodia is an odd transitional justice case because there hasn't been much of a political transition. Hun Sen was in power before, and he's still in power. If anything, his power has been consolidated and fortified. So my prediction is that it's going to take a very long time and probably the deaths of some more top Khmer Rouge leaders before it feels safe enough to broach the issue of responsibility. But this doesn't mean that there aren't a lot of other issues that can be tackled.

There needs to be exploration of positive images and sources of Cambodian identity and responses to the Khmer Rouge. The story of the resisters has never been told—the stories of the Khmer Rouge who didn't do the extra bit of evil that they had license to do. People make these distinctions, saying "Oh, she was a group leader, but she wasn't bad" or "She was a group leader, and she was evil."

Among the most important social and political events in Cambodia were the peace marches, led by a charismatic monk who mobilized hundreds of thousands of Cambodians to walk through mined territory between the Khmer Rouge zone and Phnom Penh for five consecutive years during the war.

This is a country, unfortunately, as one Cambodian said to me, where we don't have many Desmond Tutus. But the human rights community fills some of this gap. Tasks that lie ahead are creating the record and laying the foundation for memory. The most important task ahead is disarming, defusing, or at least limiting, the powerful negative themes that were the banners of the Khmer Rouge and continue to be the banners of the most destructive political forces in Cambodia: xenophobia, national imperilment, and imminent extinction.

Tribunals: Only As Good As Their Information

Iván Székely: I can share with you some comments on the problem of setting up a tribunal, a working tribunal, from the point of view of information.

Sometimes we need to report on failures. I have a feeling that the members of the human rights community, including NGOs, advocates, and activists, are overly success-oriented. We like to report on our own successes. We don't like to analyze our failures.

We are all natural allies, whether we're from the Green Movement or from movements to protect minority-group members. In reality, and especially in our region, we may sometimes feel that we are competing against each other, because we live on the same physical and nonphysical resources.

But let me draw your attention to one aspect of human rights work I find very important: information.

If you want to set up a workable international tribunal or truth and reconciliation commission, you need information, not just physical evidence. You need the facts surrounding grave violations of human rights. You need information on the victims, on the individuals. You need information on the workings of other tribunals and commissions.

Let's begin with the last one, because it would seem to be the simplest. You can read international law and read reports about the workings of tribunals. And you can form your own opinions and make your own criticism of them. These tribunals and other international bodies are usually set up for a limited duration. And, even if they work efficiently at the beginning, by the end of their mandates they begin to be uncomfortable for political and other reasons. The UN and all the other international bodies are also success-oriented. Tribunals are tempted to write quick reports about their successes. These reports are sent to the UN and locked in a repository. Nobody will have access to the real facts, to the information.

I will mention some practical initiatives by the Open Society Archives aimed at countering the practice of piling up bundles of thick reports to no real effect. We are trying to set up an international repository for information on crimes of war. We have exchanged letters with the tribunals and truth commissions, of course. And we have received kind replies, but so far not a single page of information. Of course, we don't want to take the originals. These belong to the history of the particular country, especially when the country has a memory crisis, in the sense that Dinah just used.

Let me mention two recent initiatives aimed at gathering information on war crimes from sources that have been cooperative, the NGOs and other institutions that collect such materials. One is an Open Society Archives initiative aimed at setting up a loose federation of human rights archives and documentation centers. It is designed to make people aware of the documents that exist in far-flung locations. It is not aimed at exchanging documents, but simply referencing them.

The other important initiative is a project called Martus, which belongs to a socially responsible American for-profit company called Benetech. Martus is the Latin word for "witness." This initiative is using computers and the Internet to set up a bulletin board for NGOs in order to report on the facts surrounding violations of human rights. Hopefully, our archives will be considered as a trusted third party. So we will host a Martus server.

Another part is information about the victims as individuals. This is the most problematic part. Dinah didn't mention this problem. But I know Cambodia belongs to the Eastern Hemisphere in the cultural sense of the word, and individuality has a different meaning in that part of the world. And perhaps the concept is too Western for this situation. But if you, for example, gather information for a properly set-up tribunal, you can easily violate the rights of those persons whose rights we want to protect. And this is a danger. Human rights activism is sometimes connected with collective rights. Sometimes the necessity of protecting individual rights comes up against opening information on large-scale violations of human rights.

Even if we are talking about groups of people and violations against people belonging to certain minorities or ethnic groups, the violations always affect the individual. To my mind, we should never sacrifice the victims, the survivors, the tortured, the raped, for the sake of the truth, or for the sake of justice, against their will.

This is a delicate problem. I have no simple solution for it. But when we collect information on individuals and feed this information to tribunals, we must be careful. The question is, of course, may we use these people and these pieces of information about the victims as a weapon in the cause of human rights activism, in the cause of opening up the past and showing the responsibility of persons to avoid the memory-crisis situation Dinah just described.

Dissidents and the FBI's Surveillance Files

Gara LaMarche: The sets of issues you've just described are pretty universal and difficult. Let's open it up to a broader discussion based on the experiences of people in other countries, and indeed in the United States.

In 1977, Aryeh Neier, who was then director of the American Civil Liberties Union, asked me, a 22-year-old new employee, to spend the summer in a back room reading recently obtained files from the Federal Bureau of Investigation. These files contained the results of the surveillance on the ACLU for 50 or 60 years. What was particularly interesting was the FBI's surveillance of dissidents in civil rights organizations in the United States. This was itself a human rights violation. And it posed a number of issues for the ACLU. In addition to the FBI's own crimes and the complicity of various ACLU officials in the 1940s and 1950s with the FBI, Aryeh had to grapple with the question of what was fair to the people involved.

As the files of various police agencies in a number of countries in Eastern and Central Europe have been opened up, all these questions have emerged. On the one hand, what is fair to the victims? Very often the privacy of the victims is involved. This is certainly true of any FBI file or the files of the Mississippi Sovereignty Commission and all kinds of spying agencies in the United States.

Neier was interested in the people who cooperated with the FBI and whether they wanted to offer excuses for why they did such a thing. Very often the files themselves are inherently unreliable. You're relying on some FBI agent's account to his superior of a conversation with X, which is obviously as flattering as possible to the agent and may or may not be correct with respect to X. So you have to give even the people whose files appear to show that they did something bad an opportunity to put it in some context. There are fairness issues, both to victims and to alleged perpetrators.

And these issues have emerged in every country that has had to grapple with this problem. I'm not sure I heard much in what Dinah had to say that would give any comfort to the wandering souls. What I want to ask you is what would constitute a success? Is there any reasonable basis to think that something like a tribunal or a truth commission will actually emerge in Cambodia?

Dinah PoKempner: I don't know whether something like this is going to emerge. I was a big international tribunal proponent. I still think it is critically important, in dealing with the Khmer Rouge's past, to see a process that involves punishment. To be fair, however, having examined an analysis of the evidence gathered so far against the Khmer Rouge, I don't think that it's an easy case to make.

Steve Heder, a renowned Cambodia scholar, and Brian Tittemore, a legal scholar at American University, have published a paper on the case against seven significant Khmer Rouge leaders. It was an effort to jumpstart the tribunal process, to provoke political pressure for a successful conclusion to the tribunal negotiations. But the evidence is difficult. They don't have documents that create an airtight case, for example. They have copies of documents from the central committee and regional commands. They relied in their analysis on the very controversial step of using some confessions produced under torture as evidence. An example of a less controversial use would be the fact that a memorandum or account of the confession was routed to certain leaders, establishing their likely knowledge of the torture or killing. An example of a more controversial use would be reliance on the substance of the confession on the theory it was an accurate statement before torture became so intense that victims lapsed into complete fabrication.

Whether you could pull off successful prosecutions that in all ways respect the human rights of defendants or not, it is still unlikely we're going to see the kind of tribunal that satisfies Cambodians. There are huge numbers of questions that are going to remain unanswered even in the best trial, because of the nature of the violations in Cambodia. If you're only looking between 1975 and 1979, you won't have the whole picture and won't answer some of the obsessive political questions that Cambodians have. Who did what to whom is not one of these obsessive questions.

In a sense, the privacy issues are not as high profile, because everybody's willing to talk, at least before a tribunal that has international integrity. It is not entirely unknown who did what to whom. The best thing to do now is to get people to talk about it. Cambodians can talk to foreigners about the Khmer Rouge years, because foreigners usually produce the appropriate emotional responses. They look horrified and sympathetic. If Cambodians talk about it to other Cambodians, the people on the other side of the conversation might have the reaction; "I don't want to relive this. I went through it myself. So shut up." These recountings are traumatic, and need facilitation.

So, establishing a forum where people can talk today is important. One very good project in the tribunal debate was a series of town meetings that took place throughout the country. At these meetings, people discussed whether or not there should be a tribunal. It was a moment for Khmer Rouge and others to confront each other in conversation. Both psychological and emotional issues can be confronted, and these can help people deal with the consequences of the Khmer Rouge years and probably improve coexistence or reduce tensions. There are other kinds of projects that can build memory. These projects might create the source materials for a future generation of historians to document the era and its crimes. Video documentaries, taped oral histories or survivor narratives would be useful, given that more than half the population is illiterate and newspapers have very shallow penetration nationally. The materials produced by these projects can also be drawn on by Cambodia's filmmakers.

We are talking about a process of social reconstruction that can't happen within the lifetimes of the main perpetrators.

Daniela Raiman, M.A. student in Legal Studies, CEU: You were talking about what is needed to reconstruct memories and build a history of the events in Cambodia. You were also saying that most of the people doing the writing are outside Cambodia and that there are few people in the country who are doing it. How do people in Cambodia view the works written outside the country in relation to the work written inside it? Are there any differences in how Cambodians view them? Do they correspond to the memories of the people who survived and are still living in Cambodia?

Dinah PoKempner: The survivor literature is written by people who actually lived through the Khmer Rouge years but managed to get out of the camps in Thailand in 1979 and 1980. These are people who managed to go abroad and start lives and then wrote about their childhood or what they witnessed. Their works have been written mostly in foreign languages and published by Western publishers. These works are now being translated for sale in Cambodia. But there is no real book publishing industry in Cambodia and almost no bookstores because the literacy rate is so low.

Cambodia hasn't even regained the levels of education and prosperity it had in the 1960s when secondary education was fairly common. There was a large middle class and a much richer society then.

David Rohde: What happened with the ACLU files?

Gara LaMarche: We documented instances of government surveillance of the ACLU and instances of officials of the 1940s and 1950s who cooperated with the FBI. The worst case was a fellow named Irving Ferman, who had been the director of the ACLU Washington office and had a pipeline to J. Edgar Hoover. He would, for example, feed the FBI minutes of the meetings of various ACLU chapters believed to be left-influenced. There actually was a Communist Party in the United States in the 1930s and 1940s, and it would try to infiltrate ACLU chapters. So we're not talking about something that was totally fictitious. But this does not excuse the behavior of ACLU officials.

We gave the officials involved the opportunity to look at the records and comment. Then we released it all to the press. There was a transparency about it. The story was on the front page of the *New York Times* in the summer of 1977. We all feared that the ACLU's reputation would be harmed, but it didn't seem to be. Then we set up a commission, chaired by Ramsey Clark, who had been the U.S. attorney general. In the report, the ACLU came to terms with itself, regarding both the complicity of the government and the ACLU members.

VII.

The Milosevic Trial

Moderator: *Gara LaMarche*
Speaker: *Fred Abrahams*
Comments: *Ivan Vejvoda*, executive director,
Fund for an Open Society-Serbia

Gara LaMarche: We are going to conclude the theme of "coming to terms" with a discussion of the trial of Slobodan Milosevic.

Fred Abrahams: The trial of Slobodan Milosevic is, we would all agree, historic and groundbreaking, both legally and politically. It is an important moment. I support the process fully, and I must state for the record that I worked at the tribunal on the Kosovo case. But despite all this, I am now about to shred it to pieces.

The Milosevic indictment, which named four persons along with him, came on May 27, 1999. The original indictment focused only on Kosovo, due to a problem of access to information. But it was later amended to include counts stemming from the wars in Bosnia and Croatia. The first problem that I had with the indictment was the timing. It occurred in the midst of the NATO bombing and smacked of political interference. There was, I think, a legitimate concern that this was NATO's justice. I'm not sure that there is any real validity to this. But perceptions are extremely important in the Balkans, as they are everywhere. And the perception of the tribunal as an independent, legitimate legal body was at least brought into question.

The next important moment came in October 2000, when the United States Congress passed the 2001 Foreign Operations Assistance Act. This law set a deadline. If the authorities in Yugoslavia did not fully cooperate with the war crimes tribunal and hand over indicted individuals by March 31, 2001, foreign aid to Yugoslavia would be blocked. Milosevic's arrest took place on April 1. I believe it was late in the evening. So there was no question of a direct link. I don't think anyone in Washington would deny this. But, again, it brings into question the independence of the court. People connected Milosevic's arrest with outside pressure, specifically from Washington.

The initial charges Milosevic faced in Yugoslavia had nothing to do with war crimes. He was arrested, essentially, for corruption. So, clearly, the Serbian government was nervous about this and didn't take the full step. But the political pressure from outside, particularly from Washington, continued. And Milosevic was transferred to The Hague on June 28.

I was not at Human Rights Watch at the time. But it and other organizations applied a lot of pressure on Washington to keep the pressure on Belgrade. And we should recognize that this strong lobbying effort was problematic. Again, it tainted the perception that the tribunal is independent. I'm sure that Ivan can talk about the perceptions of the tribunal in Belgrade. But clearly there's a notion that it is NATO's court.

The trial itself has, in some ways, been a very satisfying moment, certainly for me and for all of us who've worked in the Balkans or who are working on these issues in general. It's also provided some wonderful theatre. I would like to mention that you can watch the trial live on the ICTY's website. Bard College, which has a human rights program, is also posting the video the next day, so you can watch the proceedings anytime.

Milosevic's Strategy: Intimidation of Witnesses

Milosevic has not recognized the legitimacy of the court and has not appointed a lawyer. He is not cooperating with the friends of the court that the judges appointed for him. Instead, he has been conducting his own defense, which has created some very unique dynamics. First of all, it allows Milosevic more leeway, because he is cross-examining witnesses himself. The judges have given him a little more space than they would allow a defense attorney under normal circumstances. It also allows him—and I believe this was a part of his strategy—to intimidate witnesses. He's arrogant. He's bullying. He's posturing. And he's intimidating.

But I think the witnesses are beginning to get a feel for him. They are getting used to the game. At the beginning, it was difficult for people. Early on, a Kosovar Albanian villager, a farmer, began to cry on the stand. He couldn't go on and asked to be excused. There was also very interesting testimony from an officer of the OSCE mission in Kosovo, a British soldier, I think, who was responsible for liasing with the Yugoslav military. He testified that, during a private conversation, a Yugoslav Army official told him, "You know, we have this plan. If you bomb, we're going to cleanse Kosovo." Of course, Milosevic challenged it. During the challenge, he said, "We'll find out who this guy is and who his family is." The impact this can have on potential insiders is clear, if and when any former Serbian official comes forward to talk about dirty, backroom deals. Obviously, having to face this man, who knows all the dirty laundry that he knows, can be intimidating.

Milosevic has also tried to discredit witnesses by craftily using information. Where this information comes from is not known. But he has shown a very intimate knowledge of the witnesses. After one Kosovar Albanian testified about crimes in his region, Milosevic asked, "Isn't it true that your brother was arrested for rape in 1985?" I'm not sure of the dates, but that was the essence of the accusation, which was true. He also asked other very specific questions, things like "Isn't it true that in this village these four houses were destroyed in the 1998 offensive. So how was it possible that you didn't have a clear view of the road?" Questions of this nature reveal very intimate knowledge.

There has been a lot of speculation in Belgrade about where he's getting this information. Some people say he took intelligence files with him when he left office. Others say he has a network of people who want to help him and are calling in the information. I don't know the answer.

It is clear that this trial has two streams, the legal stream and the political. The prosecution is pursuing the legal approach to secure a conviction. But Milosevic is playing a political game. This is obvious. The best example I can give relates, again, to the Kosovar Albanian villagers who have testified. They have shown an amnesia about KLA (Kosovo Liberation Army) activity. When Milosevic cross-examines them, he asks, "Isn't it true that the KLA was in your village?" They answer, "Well, I never saw them," which says nothing about their real knowledge of KLA crimes.

My colleague at Human Rights Watch, Bogdan Ivanisevic, wrote something that highlights the legal-political schism in the Milosevic trial. On the one hand, politically, with witnesses like this, Milosevic is scoring solid points in Belgrade: You see these guys. They say they don't know anything. They're not going to talk about the KLA. And this is perceived as a bias of the court and so on. Legally speaking, on the other hand, there may be some argument. It undermines a witness's credibility if he or she claims not to know about something that was going on in their village. But it doesn't have such an impact because, basically, the crimes of the KLA do not excuse the actions of the accused. So, even these attempts by the defendant do not do much to strengthen his legal case. We're seeing that he's not pursuing a strategy with an acquittal in mind. He is playing to the home crowd. He is trying to secure his place in history as the defender of the Serb nation against the larger international conspiracy.

So, how will the trial proceed? I don't know. A key question will be whether one of the so-called insiders will come forward to testify. This is what everybody's waiting for. Last week, for instance, some important people were again under pressure from the United States government. More indicted people surrendered willingly, including the head of the Yugoslav Army, Dragoljub Ojdanic, and a very important person, the deputy prime minister, Nikola Sainovic. Whether they will turn on their former boss or not is a question. Whether they can plea bargain is a question.

In the Kosovo case, it is interesting to consider the arguments for Milosevic's legal responsibility based upon de jure and de facto chain of command. In the Kosovo case, the de jure link is very strong. Kosovo was clearly an internal Serbian conflict. Milosevic, as president of the Federal Republic of Yugoslavia, was the head of the Supreme Defense Council, which has control of the army. So, there's a very direct de jure link that alone can get him for Kosovo. The police actions in Kosovo are more complicated, because that went through the Serbian interior ministry, and the structures of the interior ministry are far more complex. They involved parallel, hidden, and overlapping structures, many of which are still unclear. These de jure arguments will be more difficult to make in Bosnia and Croatia, because these were different countries.

A Questionable Choice of Whom to Indict

The de facto and de jure question will play a role in the trials of the co-indictees, Sainovic and Ojdanic. I believe that, for various reasons, including pressure on the tribunal to show progress, the choice of indictees was questionable. In many ways, the prosecuting attorneys went after titles. The best example of this, I think, is Ojdanic, who is widely believed to have been a crony, a rubber stamp, who didn't have his hands directly on the levers. A similar thing could be said for the minister of interior, Vlajko Stojiljkovic, who blew his brains out on the steps of Parliament. I don't know whether he'd still be alive today, whether he wouldn't have pulled the trigger, if he had known more. Perhaps.

At the same time, you still have individuals who were key players in the de facto game, people like Frenki Simatovic, the head of the JSO, a key link between the secret service and the paramilitaries, who participated in funding paramilitaries and various criminal activities. I'm also referring to Frenki's successor as the JSO leader, Milorad Lukovic. Key people like these played central roles in all three conflicts. They are still at large. And they are not named on public indictments. Why is this?

I think there was a lot of pressure on the tribunal from the outside. Once the tribunal was created, the people running it had to show progress. But, unfortunately, I think there is another factor in the poor choices of whom to indict, and it is much more mundane. It is a poor understanding of the region and the conflict. This came up in Bill's talk. And Sonja referred to journalists who know the issue and can get a little deeper and talk about causes, instead of others who show up only when a place is bleeding and leading the papers. In this regard, I must say that working at the tribunal was a somewhat disturbing experience.

One complicated problem, a problem I don't have a real answer for, is how the tribunal deals with locals, in this case the citizens of the former Yugoslavia. It is an issue that the International Criminal Court is going to have to grapple with. There is a policy against hiring people from the region except for working on open sources or, obviously, translating. I can understand the justification for this policy, but there also needs to be some balance. There is a need for knowledgeable people, good people, experts on the security structures, for example, who can at least act in an advisory capacity. I can tell you horrible stories. My favorite, which I chuckle at even though it is actually quite sad, involves an investigator from the tribunal who called down to the analyst's room and said, "Listen, I just have a quick question for you about Banja Luka." Banja Luka, one of the towns in Bosnia. But the investigator asked, "Well, what's that Banja Luka? Is it a man or a woman?"

If you go down to the first floor of the tribunal, there's a library. Sadly, many of the books have no crease in the spine. In fact, there is a belief among some investigators that it is better not to know the region, that knowledge of the region means that you might approach it with a bias. And I think the investigations reflect this. I was not a part of the Bosnia investigations. I'm a little hesitant to say too much about it, because I just don't know much. But I was told by colleagues there that because of this poor understanding of the region, investigators tended to rush to Bosnia without any sort of investigative strategy. Some of them are very qualified policemen from Australia, Germany, Pakistan, and so on. But the worst crime they had ever seen might have involved a local drug dealer shot on some corner. These guys rushed into Bosnia and said, "Oh, my God, eight people were killed here." Then they spent a lot of time and resources looking into this incident instead of incidents that were a lot more significant. This is one of the reasons certain cases were chosen. Some were chosen apparently randomly, because the decisions stemmed from a lack of strategy, which comes from a lack of understanding.

I am also concerned that the ICTY is divorced from the region, that the ICTY is not organically linked to the region. I am concerned that there are two agendas: the local agenda of justice and accountability, perhaps leading to reconciliation, and a UN agenda, or this international, let's say ICTY agenda. The two need to be better harmonized. It would be interesting to hear about the tribunal's impact on local courts, for example, and how local war crimes investigations are going to proceed.

I will close with two points to put this in context. The first point involves the investigations of the KLA and NATO. The prosecutor has stated publicly that they are investigating the KLA. Carla Del Ponte was in Pristina last week and said, "You can expect something soon." There is a lot of pressure on her to bring indictments against members of the KLA. It is a big betting game in Pristina now. Everyone is turning around to friends who are former members of the KLA and saying, "Don't worry, you were a small fish." But that's a problem, because the structure of the KLA is complicated. It's questionable that the KLA even exists as a vertical organization. It had more of a horizontal structure. So finding the link to the bigger people is going to be difficult. And if you don't find it, you're going to be stuck with the commander from a town of 80,000 people and Milosevic. So, there's an issue there that needs to be resolved.

Lastly: NATO. Amnesty International came out with a report claiming that NATO had committed war crimes during its operations against Serbia and Montenegro. Human Rights Watch came out with a report saying that NATO had violated international humanitarian law by not taking adequate precautions to minimize civilian casualties but that this did not cross the threshold of a war crime. I think the key issue is the question of criminal intent. There was negligence on NATO's part, but there wasn't criminal intent to target civilians. In any case, the prosecutor's office conducted a preliminary investigation and determined that further investigation wasn't required. The ICTY made a very conservative legal interpretation in reaching this conclusion. This is paradoxical and contradictory. While the prosecution is welcoming progressive interpretations by the court about the gray areas of international humanitarian law, it took a very conservative position regarding the possible investigation of NATO. Basically they closed the door on these inquiries.

So I believe there is some validity to the criticisms coming from Belgrade. I think that they should be taken into consideration when thinking about the International Criminal Court. One of these criticisms is that Western governments largely fund the tribunal. Secondly, the prosecutor's office was, and still is, reliant upon on intelligence from NATO governments. There are investigative limitations. There needs to be some cooperation, not to mention more arrests of the persons indicted.

Gara LaMarche: Ivan Vejvoda made me think of a book I'm reading now by my former colleague at Human Rights Watch, Jeri Laber. She's written the memoirs of her work in Eastern Europe in the early 1980s, where she learned to evade the police by taking her notes in handwriting so small they could only be read with a magnifying glass. I don't know if Ivan has had that kind of practice, but in any event, if they fall into other hands, you're very safe.

Yugoslavia: Open Fractures of the Soul

Ivan Vejvoda: I was really struck, being of an older generation than the others here, by what Dinah said about books in Cambodia and their lack of availability, the lack of bookshops. It's something so striking for us who grew up in the 1960s and knew about Phnom Penh. Yugoslavs who'd been there came back and said it was such a beautiful town. The immediate association I had involved the third or fourth week of bombing during the NATO intervention. Sonja will recall this because we were together. A colleague of ours, the program coordinator, came into the office just before we were going to go home. We usually left about five o'clock because the sirens would go off between six and seven, and we would be with our families for the night. She brought the Serbian translation of Hannah Arendt's *The Origins of Totalitarianism*. I said, "My gosh, this is such a paradox. Here we are in this situation, and yet this book is being published very normally." I bought many copies for friends who were unable to read it earlier in English.

When people would ask me why Milosevic gave up in the end, the one word I came up with was "Europe." There is a geographical context to this. You know why we have a trial on the former Yugoslavia and why we don't have one for the poor Sudanese and the two million nobody talks about. It has to do with Europe. The association I have is the "Never again" association.

We were brought up with the "Never again" story from our days in elementary school. It was shoved down our throats through high school and through university. We were taken to this town where the Nazis killed 6,000 kids and their high school teachers in 1941. German tourists could not enter that town until the 1960s because 6,000 kids were killed there in one day. We were so naive as social scientists. I never believed we would go to war, in the middle of Europe after what happened after 1945. It was such a shocker to all of us. How could you squander 50 years of rather enlightened communism, with all of its faults? We were, at the time, first in line to enter Europe. We had relations with the European Community that went back to 1970. There were negotiations in Brussels in December of 1990 to take the next step.

Bill's account of Africa rang so many bells for me. What happened in Yugoslavia is exactly the same as what he described. I described this syndrome in a rather modest book I published with a friend in England. It was a power-retention strategy. As the Berlin Wall fell in 1989, you had eight communist elites in Yugoslavia's six republics and two autonomous provinces. They felt the wind of globalization. They knew they would not be able to retain their Mercedes and their villas and their high salaries in a reformed democratized country. Let me, the individual naive democrat who had felt very bad about that communism since the late 1970s, take some individual responsibility. I and friends like Sonja thought we were going to make it into the third Yugoslavia–after the first, monarchist Yugoslavia and the second, communist Yugoslavia. Finally, we were going to be the first communist country to enter the European Union and to be able to indulge in whatever, *Baywatch, Sex in the City*–and get on with life.

It didn't happen that way. And that wonderful expression: wandering souls. A Yugoslav, a Belgrade playwright, wrote that we had open fractures of the soul. You can't see them. But you can feel them. We lost a country, again, in the middle of Europe. And that's why Milosevic is in the right place. Whatever the faults of the tribunal are, and there are many—and we discuss them every day.

The other element of those early days of the Milosevic trial was the spectator-sport element. Mr. X against the rest of the world. Like everywhere else, people back home watched to see how Mr. X was going to deal with it. And he fared quite well. He got ready for the whole thing.

So, Milosevic. We recognized him in 1983 when he became party secretary in Belgrade. We knew this was bad news. We didn't know how bad, though. Then, in 1987, when he made the party coup and took over from Ivan Stambolic in Serbia, we knew it was getting worse. But again, you know, it didn't look that bad. We had seen worse times.

So, we have been vindicated by where he is. When he was arrested and transferred, there was a deep sense of relief in the country, in society. I would say that, on balance, public opinion and the so-called street-wise person are more mature than our politicians in this sense. They know deep down what he did and how he abused them and the country. He brought out tanks against us, the citizens of Belgrade, on March 9, 1991, before any war had started. I took my five-year-old son the next day to see those tanks. Maybe he would remember some of it. Milosevic lasted too long for a European country. That was the problem.

We thought we had him on March 9, 1991. The students invited him to the Rector's Palace at Belgrade University. On March 12, they told him everything that would happen and that he was a bastard. He sat there and listened with sort of the same face and chin up that he has in the tribunal. He listened to everything these students had to say. They very courageously spoke up against him, then he left and continued. But he overplayed his hand, played one bridge too far for him. There wouldn't have been an indictment had he signed at Rambouillet, and the deal at Rambouillet was wonderful compared with the deal he got later on.

As usual, for these kinds of dictators, like Mobutu and others, they can't feel where the limit is. They're like children testing out the limits. Then they go too far. Milosevic was something some of us recognized very early on, something others recognized as we went on, and something, finally, only after the bombing, more or less everybody recognized. The writing was on the wall. This was a dead-end street. He had to go. In that sense, with the tribunal, there's no major problem.

A Legacy of Shades of Grey

The pressure from abroad. I must say the reformist politicians in Serbia don't deny the pressure. Colin Powell has said we need a reasonable kind of pressure along with some carrots. The reformist politicians understand that you have to be under a deadline to submit your papers at university. That's why the deadline's there. It's a condition. It's pressure. The professor doesn't say to hand in your paper whenever you want. He says, "May 1." That's the kind of thing that is needed.

This is first of all important because of the legacy. It would be much easier to say, "Look, it's a black-and-white picture that the West's been telling us. Let's go home and look to the future." But the picture is really all those shades of gray. And the shades of gray have a lot to do with our legacy. It's a very difficult legacy of an agrarian, paternalistic, patriarchal society–a collectivist mentality. We haven't moved to individualism yet.

Yes, we watch *Sex in the City* at ten in the evening. But we're still not New York-style individuals yet. We're still in that collective mindset. That's one thing. Then there's the legacy of communism, which was happy to marry the agrarian, paternalistic, patriarchal legacy. On top of this you get Milosevic, you get the traumatized society, and the legacy of general disablement, of an atomized, fragmentized society from communism.

What was the silver lining of the decade under Milosevic? This society actually started coming together. It started to become more individualistic. The civil society, with a little help from our friends outside and the independent media, had to pull itself up by its own bootstraps.

This is the great story, I would say. It is the untold story that goes along with the catastrophe. And that's why it's so great. This regime of Milosevic is work for political theory and sociology. I mean, we always could speak out whenever we wanted. It was dangerous and risky. Some people ended up in jail. Others were killed. But papers came out. Veton Surroi was published. So it was a very strange system, terribly authoritarian, terribly oppressive, apartheid in Kosovo, such a muddle.

For people who are unsophisticated analytically, it was hard to understand what this was all about. I think it's very important to understand the whole rainbow of diversity that existed. Belgrade remained the multicultural city that it always was. Two million people. I am from a mixed family. Sonja is whatever she is. A lot of our friends are Croats and Muslims. We survived. We were not kicked out of our jobs as many of our Serb friends in Zagreb were. It was very mixed, very muddled. This is where a lot of the unease comes from. And it is then focused on the tribunal, because the tribunal simplifies things necessarily, by virtue of its own field of activity.

On the trial itself, on justice itself, I think the tribunal has a place in a broader structure. There is the issue of the jurisdiction, of justice, and that has an international level and a domestic level. And there's the much broader, more difficult dynamic of society coming to terms with itself. These are, of course, related things. But they are also very separate things. We know this from Germany, from Latin America, from Spain, and Portugal. Our problem, or advantage, was that we nearly scraped through with pushing the past under the carpet in 1945. But, unfortunately, we didn't. So we can't repeat that experience now, because we know that pushing it under the carpet doesn't work. It caught up with us 50 years later. So we have to take the more difficult but, hopefully, the more successful road of actually coming to terms and confronting the past.

This is where the tribunal has its role, but only as one element. We also have to go to the domestic side. I think this will evolve slowly as we go through transition and reform, and especially the judicial section will be part of this transition and reform. It will be very difficult. There is a lack of money. There are questions about the opening up of the files. All this is on the table and very publicly discussed.

We were both in a conference a month ago on the files. The minister of police was there talking very openly about the options, about all the problems with files that Gara was mentioning. How much is true in the files? How do you handle this very sensitive material? There is a willingness to move to the courts, to the domestic courts.

Ideally we would be trying Milosevic in Belgrade in the presence of The Hague tribunal—a doubles act, if you will, but on domestic territory—because I think it would be better for society to watch him being confronted with these charges at home. We seek public acknowledgment there, public recognition that this happened. This has to do with the whole information strategy. Now a lot of things are going on in regard to information. The Central European University Press has translated and published a book called *The Road to War in Serbia*. It is the work of people, of friends and colleagues, who from 1991, as soon as the war began, started analyzing why this war happened. And what they've found brings us back to Hannah Arendt, to understanding and analyzing the deep causes: Why did we plunge ourselves into this? The book was first published in the middle of the war, I think in 1995 or 1996. The Serbian title is *The Serbian Side of the War.* This was already the beginning of the process of society coming to terms with itself.

There are much broader activities. There are documentation centers, public TV programs. You can watch the tribunal live on the B92 website every day. So there is access to this information.

By and large, domestic journalists are not doing such a good job, because they are not sufficiently trained and they are talking more to the lawyers and the indicted than to the prosecution or to the judges. There are also a lot of public events, very heated debates. Both sides come. They share the kind of things we've heard all along, all these stories: somebody out there wants to annihilate the Serbian soul basically. That's the kind of thing, and these people who understand that they have to push this agenda forward very strongly.

It's a very mixed picture, a muddled picture. I wouldn't say it's chaotic. It's simply like the Big Bang. All the elements are there, but they haven't coalesced yet. We are into the second year of the transition. And as in every transition, if you go back to 1990 or 1991 in Poland or Hungary, things are not clear. But, for us who are inside, the ship is on course. The winds are battering it from left and right. The waves are very high. But somehow the ship keeps going.

Continuing Corruption, But a Willingness to Reform

The corruption issue is still huge, that remnant of the old guard. And I think Milosevic is getting information from inside. There are pockets within the military and police that haven't been touched yet. These people have access to some of this information and are feeding it to him. Many of the ministries have been attacked from the top. So until you get to the basement, where the books are, it takes a lot of time. But I think that there is a willingness. The whole reform of the law enforcement side, the police and military and judiciary and public administration, all this has been launched. But because you're launching it simultaneously, you're moving very slowly. The public's response for the moment, to generalize, is still patience. There have been important strikes and unrest of sorts. But if you take two steps back and you look at how it's happening, you see that, by and large, it's moving. Within this context, I would say that if the tribunal indicted two or three people from the KLA who have allegedly committed war crimes, I think it would alleviate some of the misperceptions about the tribunal. It would be helpful for all those people who are advocating the necessity of the tribunal even with all of its deficiencies.

Samantha Power: I never thought, all these years later, it could be so stimulating to listen to talk of Milosevic. I guess that's what makes him what he is.

It seems to me that the criticisms of the tribunal uttered over the last nine years are warranted. This is especially true of the issue of selectivity, the selectivity of an ad hoc tribunal, of a tribunal for the former Yugoslavia for a whole set of political reasons, and giving rise in the legal mission creep to the tribunal in Rwanda. But this was very much a product of the problem that arises when, having just set up a tribunal for the former Yugoslavia, you have 800,000 people killed in Rwanda.

Then there's the form of selectivity Judge Wald talked about: selectivity in terms of whom you pick up. It seems to me that one of the things we should be very careful, or even reluctant, to criticize is the inherent selectivity of the pressure put on Serbia, Croatia, and Bosnia—the idea that we should be nervous if Western governments are putting pressure on states to turn over indictees. It seems to me that—given that it's the norm that we do not apply any pressure—this is an exceptional situation. One of Sonja's criticisms was aimed at the Bush administration's announcement that the tribunal should wrap up its work by 2008. I think this is very important. It touches on Dinah's point about the positive stories and about not overdoing things as we critique this very flawed but very necessary institution.

The tribunal is an international institution. It is not a transnational institution. It doesn't have a standing army of its own. And until George Soros decides to create one, we're stuck with the member states. And until Ireland develops a military and economic capacity like that of the United States, we're also stuck with the major powers that we have, soiled hands and all.

We're in the room with people who know the situation in former Yugoslavia and in Belgrade so much better than we do as outsiders who think of ourselves as well meaning. I think there's a temptation to be very deferential in a politically correct way. To say that, "We understand that Western governments have pressed your regime and interfered with your sovereignty. But you forfeit sovereignty at a certain point when certain abuses are being committed." Now, as we correctly critique the tribunal, we should not take it as a given that just because it's international, it's good, or just because it has Slobo Milosevic in custody, it's good. We need state power, unfortunately, until we live in a different world. What is Human Rights Watch to do but pressure the U.S. government to pressure Serbia?

Fred Abrahams: I would perhaps clarify this. I understand your point and I agree with it. I was among those people advocating, strongly, for Washington to keep that pressure on Serbia. I guess what I was trying to say is that we should also recognize the imperfections, especially with regard to the perceptions they create. Was this the only road now? Yes. But can we still analyze it and think of ways to mitigate these problems in the future? I think we can and should. Ultimately, this is a big debate. What are the goals of the tribunal? I would hope that one of the goals is to help establish a secure environment in the former Yugoslavia, to establish some accountability so that this society can heal and move on. And if this is the case, if this is our goal, then we have to consider how this process is viewed from that side. I'm not saying we should let that dictate how we should proceed. But we have to at least think about it.

The Price of Permitting This Horrible Evil

Ivan Vejvoda: To be thoroughly blunt, the way that I speak to taxi drivers about the tribunal, I say, "You simply do not do something like this at the end of the 20th century in the middle of Europe with Christiane Amanpour around. This is the price that you have to pay now for doing something that you shouldn't have done. It's counter to every historical dynamic of Europe. This is the price you have to pay just to remain on this continent after everything that has happened, and because you were forgetting that the world is an imperfect place, that there is no universal justice, and that not everyone will be using silk gloves. This is what you have to go through to expiate what you did and shouldn't have done. And it is not nice. The pressures are out there, you have to relinquish your sovereignty. You know 15 European countries have relinquished their sovereignty. So why not you, who have permitted, as a society, all of this horrible evil."

We feel shame that this European country has allowed itself to go through this. This is the imperfect way that we are going to muddle ourselves out.

David Rohde: But is the taxi driver listening to you or to Milosevic's political appeal? Is the story that Milosevic is telling in the trial selling?

Ivan Vejvoda: It's not selling really. It's not selling.

Sonja Licht: Some are listening to this, some are listening to that.

Gara LaMarche: And the rest are watching *Baywatch*.

Ivan Vejvoda: Most in fact. As somebody said, you can't get up every morning and think of what a terrible thing my society has done. You have to earn your bread that day. It's linked to economic and social stability, of course. I think we would be doing more confronting and coming to terms with ourselves if our salaries were a little better.

Gara LaMarche: It's a very strange world we live in. When we were talking about "never again," I was thinking about something I read a couple of weeks ago in a column by Thomas L. Friedman of the *New York Times*. He was writing from Israel about an acquaintance. There was a suicide bombing near the home of a friend of Friedman's acquaintance, at a cafe where his daughter hung out. Friedman apparently asked the man whether his daughter was safe. The man answered, "Thank God, she's in Auschwitz." She was on a school trip visiting the Auschwitz site. She had avoided being killed because she was in Auschwitz. So, a world where Auschwitz can be normalized is a strange place.

Suggested Readings

Abella, Rosalie Silberman, Warren Allmand, and Ruth Wedgwood. 2000. Hate, genocide and human rights fifty years later: What have we learned? What must we do? *McGill Law Journal* 46 (1): 105.

Abrahams, Fred, Eric Stover, and Gilles Peress. 2001. *A village destroyed, May 14, 1999: War crimes in Kosovo.* Berkeley: University of California Press.

Abrams, Jason. 2001. The atrocities in Cambodia and Kosovo: Observations on the codification of genocide. *New England Law Review* 35 (2): 303-310.

Adelman, Howard, and Astri Suhrke, eds. 1999. *The path of a genocide: The Rwanda crisis from Uganda to Zaire.* New Brunswick, NJ: Transaction Publishers.

Adhoc, Licadho, and Human Rights Watch. 1999. *Impunity in Cambodia: How Human Rights Offenders Escape Justice.* New York: Human Rights Watch.

Afflitto, Frank M. 2000. Victimization, survival and the impunity of forced exile: A case study from the Rwandan genocide. *Crime, Law and Social Change* 34: 77-97.

Allen, Tim, and Jean Seaton, eds. 1999. *The media of conflict: War reporting and representations of ethnic violence.* London and New York: Zed Books.

Alston, Philip, and James Crawford. 2000. *The future of UN human rights treaty monitoring.* Cambridge: Cambridge University Press.

Alvarez, Alex. 2001. *Governments, citizens, and genocide: A comparative and interdisciplinary approach.* Bloomington: Indiana University Press.

Alvarez, Jose E. 1999. Crimes of states/crimes of hate: Lessons from Rwanda. *The Yale Journal of International Law* 39 (2): 365-483.

Amann, Diane Marie. 1999. Prosecutor v. Akayesu—Judgment by International Criminal Tribunal for Rwanda on charges of genocide and international crimes of sexual violence. *The American Journal of International Law* 93:195.

American Psychological Association. 2000. *Ethnopolitical warfare: Causes, consequences, and possible solutions*. Washington, DC: American Psychological Association.

Amnesty International. 2000. *Amnesty International Report, 2000*.

Andreopoulos, George J. 2002. *Concepts and strategies in international human rights*. New York: Lang.

Anglin, Douglas G. 2002. *Confronting Rwandan genocide: The military options: What could and should the international community have done?* Clementsport, N.S.: Canadian Peacekeeping Press.

Anzulovic, Branimir. 1999. *Heavenly Serbia: From myth to genocide*. London: Hurst & Co.

Arbour, Louise. 1999. The prosecution of international crimes: Prospects and pitfalls. *Washington University Journal of Law and Policy* 1:13-25.

Ashmore, Richard D., and Lee J. Jussim. 2001. *Social identity, intergroup conflict, and conflict reduction*. Oxford and New York: Oxford University Press.

Association of Genocide Scholars. 1999. *Genocide: Essays toward understanding, early-warning, and prevention*. Williamsburg, VA: Association of Genocide Scholars.

Atwood, J. Brian. 1999. Early warning and prevention of genocide and crimes against humanity. *Journal of Intergroup Relations* 26 (2): 32.

Bacevich, Andrew J., and Eliot A. Cohen. 2001. *War over Kosovo*. New York: Columbia University Press.

Baehr, Peter R. 2001. *Human rights: Universality in practice*. London: Palgrave.

Ball, Howard. 1999. *Prosecuting war crimes and genocide: The twentieth-century experience*. Lawrence: University Press of Kansas.

Barkan, Elazar. 2000. *The guilt of nations: Restitution and negotiating historical injustices*. New York: W.W. Norton Company.

Barkan, Steven E., and Lynne L. Snowden. 2001. *Collective violence*. Boston: Allyn and Bacon.

Barnett, Michael N. 2002. *Eyewitness to a genocide: The United Nations and Rwanda*. Ithaca, NY: Cornell University Press.

Bartov, Omer. 2000. *Mirrors of destruction: War, genocide, and modern identity*. New York: Oxford University Press.

Bartov, Omer, and Atina Grossmann. 2002. *Crimes of war: Guilt and denial in the twentieth century*. New York: New Press.

Bartov, Omer, and Phyllis Mack. 2001. *In God's name: Genocide and religion in the twentieth century*. New York: Berghahn Books.

Bass, Gary Jonathan. 2000. *Stay the hand of vengeance: The politics of war crimes tribunals*. Princeton, NJ: Princeton University Press.

Bax, Mart. 2000. Warlords, priests and the politics of ethnic cleansing: A case study from rural Bosnia-Hercegovina. *Ethnic and Racial Studies* 23 (1): 16-36.

Becker, Daniel F., Stevan Weine, Dolores Vojvoda, and Thomas H. McGlashan. 1999. PTSD symptoms in adolescent survivors of ethnic cleansing. *Journal of the American Academy of Child and Adolescent Psychiatry* 38 (6): 775-782.

Becker, Elizabeth. 1998. *When the war was over: Cambodia and the Khmer Rouge revolution*. New York: PublicAffairs.

Bell-Fialkoff, Andrew. 1999. *Ethnic cleansing*. New York: St. Martin's Press/Griffin.

Berkeley, Bill. 2001. *The graves are not yet full: Race, tribe and power in the heart of Africa*. New York: Basic Books.

Berry, John A., and Carol Pott Berry, eds. 1999. *Genocide in Rwanda: A collective memory*. Washington, DC: Howard University Press.

Bhavnani, Ravi, and David Backer. 2000. Localized ethnic conflict and genocide: Accounting for differences in Rwanda and Burundi. *The Journal of Conflict Resolution* 44 (3): 283.

Biggar, Nigel. 2001. *Burying the past: Making peace and doing justice after civil conflict*. Washington, DC: Georgetown University Press.

Blessington, Daniel J. 1998. From Dayton to Sarajevo: Enforcing election law in post-war Bosnia and Herzegovina. *The American University International Law Review* 13:553.

Boed, Roman. 1999. Searching for common humanity in the context of mass violence. *Columbia Journal of Transnational Law* 38 (2):451-6.

Bolton, Paul. 2001. Local perceptions of the mental health effects of the Rwandan genocide. *Journal of Nervous and Mental Disease* 189 (4): 243-248.

Booth, Ken. 2001. *The Kosovo tragedy: The human rights dimensions*. London and Portland, OR: Frank Cass.

Bosco, David L. 1998. After genocide: Building peace in Bosnia. *The American Prospect* 39:16.

———. 1998. Reintegrating Bosnia: A progress report. *The Washington Quarterly* 21 (2): 65-81.

Brown, Cynthia G., Farhad Karim, and Human Rights Watch. 1995. *Playing the "communal card": Communal violence and human rights*. New York: Human Rights Watch.

Brown, Michael E., and Richard N. Rosecrance. 1999. *The costs of conflict: Prevention and cure in the global arena*. Washington, DC: Carnegie Commission on Preventing Deadly Conflict.

Browning, Christopher R. 1992. *Ordinary men: Reserve Police Battalion 101 and the final solution in Poland*. New York: HarperCollins.

Bugingo, François. 2000. Rwanda: Chronique d'un genocide previsible. *McGill Law Journal* 46 (1): 179-186.

Burg, Steven L., and Paul S. Shoup. 1999. *The war in Bosnia-Herzegovina: Ethnic conflict and international intervention*. Armonk, NY: M.E. Sharpe.

California Dept. of Education. 2000. *Model curriculum for human rights and genocide*. Sacramento, CA: California Dept. of Education.

Campbell, David. 1998. *National deconstruction: Violence, identity, and justice in Bosnia*. Minneapolis: University of Minnesota.

Campbell, Greg. 1999. *The road to Kosovo: A Balkan diary*. Boulder, CO: Westview Press.

Campbell, Horace. 1999. Liberation, genocide and military entrepreneurs in Africa. *Canadian Journal of African Studies* 33 (1): 155-161.

Campbell, Kenneth J. 1999. *Genocide and the global village*. Basinstoke: Macmillan.

Carey, Carlyn M. 1999. Internal displacement: Is prevention through accountability possible? A Kosovo case study. *The American University Law Review* 49:243.

Carpenter, Robyn Charli. 2000. Forced maternity, children's rights and the genocide convention: A theoretical analysis. *Journal of Genocide Research* 2 (2): 213-244.

Cernea, Michael, and Christopher McDowell. 2000. *Risks and reconstruction: Experiences of resettlers and refugees.* Washington, DC: World Bank.

Chandler, David. 1999. *Bosnia: Faking democracy after Dayton.* London: Pluto Press.

———. 2001. *From Kosovo to Kabul: Human rights and international intervention.* London and Sterling, VA: Pluto Press.

Chandler, David P. 1991. *The tragedy of Cambodian history: Politics, war, and revolution since 1945.* New Haven: Yale University Press.

———. 1999. *Brother Number One: A political biography of Pol Pot.* Boulder, CO: Westview Press.

———. 1999. *Voices from S-21: Terror and history in Pol Pot's secret prison.* Berkeley: University of California Press.

Charny, Israel W., ed., forewords by Archbishop Desmond Tutu and Simon Wiesenthal. *Encyclopedia of genocide.* Santa Barbara, CA: ABC-CLIO, 1999.

Charny, Israel W. 2000. Innocent denials of known genocides: A further contribution to a psychology of denial of genocide. *Human Rights Review* 1 (3): 15-39.

Chatterjee, Pratap. 1998. The Gold Rush legacy: Greed, pollution and genocide. *Earth Island Journal* 13:26.

Chesterman, Simon. 2000. An altogether different order: Defining the elements of crimes against humanity. *Duke Journal of Comparative & International Law* 10:307.

Chigas, George. 2000. The politics of defining justice after the Cambodian genocide. *Journal of Genocide Research* 2 (2): 245-265.

Chippendale, Neil. 2000. *Crimes against humanity.* Philadelphia: Chelsea House Publishers.

Chirot, Daniel, and Martin E.P. Seligman. 2001. *Ethnopolitical warfare: Causes, consequences, and possible solutions.* Washington, DC: American Psychological Association.

Chorbajian, Levon, and George Shirinian, eds. 1998. *Studies in comparative genocide.* New York: St. Martin's Press.

Chorbajian, Levon, and George Shirinian. 1999. Collected essays—Comparative/world—Studies in comparative genocide. *The American Historical Review* 104 (4): 1431.

Cigar, Norman, and Paul Williams. 2002. *Indictment at The Hague: The Milosevic regime and crimes of the Balkan wars.* New York: New York University Press.

Clark, Ann Marie. 2001. *Diplomacy of conscience: Amnesty International and changing human rights norms.* Princeton: Princeton University Press.

Clark, Wesley K. 2001. *Waging modern war: Bosnia, Kosovo, and the future of combat.* New York: PublicAffairs.

Cohen, Herman J. 2000. *Intervening in Africa: Superpower peacemaking in a troubled continent.* New York: Palgrave.

Cohen, Leonard. 2000. *Serpent in the bosom: The rise and fall of Slobodan Milosevic.* Boulder, CO and Oxford: Westview Press.

Cohen, Roger. 1998. *Hearts grown brutal: Sagas of Sarajevo.* New York: Random House.

Cohen, Stanley. 2001. *States of denial: Knowing about atrocities and suffering.* Cambridge, UK and Malden, MA: Blackwell Publishers.

Coker, Christopher. 2001. *Humane warfare.* New York: Routledge.

Confessore, Nicholas. 1999. State of the debate: Rwanda, Kosovo, and the limits of justice. *The American Prospect* 45:90.

Cooper, Belinda, ed. 1999. *War crimes: the legacy of Nuremberg.* New York: TV Books.

Copelon, Rhonda. 2000. Gender crimes as war crimes: Integrating crimes against women into international criminal law. *McGill Law Journal* 46:217-240.

Cox, Marcus. 1998. The right to return home: International intervention and ethnic cleansing in Bosnia and Herzegovina. *International and Comparative Law Quarterly* 47:599-631.

Coy, Patrick G., and Lynee M. Woehrle. 2000. *Social conflicts and collective identities.* Lanham, MD: Rowman & Littlefield.

Crocker, Chester A., Fen Osler Hampson, and Pamela Aall, eds. 2001. *Turbulent peace: The challenges of managing international conflict.* Washington, DC: United States Institute of Peace Press.

Daalder, Ivo H., and Michael E. O'Hanlon. 2001. *Winning ugly: NATO's war to save Kosovo.* Washington, DC: Brookings Institution Press.

D'Amato, Anthony. 1999. A brief review of the indictment against Milosevic and others. *International Peacekeeping* 5 (3): 91.

———. 2000. Defending a Person Charged with Genocide. *Chicago Journal of International Law* 1 (2): 459.

Day, L. Edward, and Margaret Vandiver. 2000. Criminology and Genocide Studies: Notes on what might have been and what still could be. *Crime, Law, and Social Change* 34:43-59.

Des Forges, Alison Liebhafsky. 1999. *Leave none to tell the story: Genocide in Rwanda.* New York and Paris: Human Rights Watch and International Federation of Human Rights.

Doder, Dusko. 1999. *Milosevic: Portrait of a tyrant.* New York: Free Press.

Doubt, Keith. 2000. *Sociology after Bosnia and Kosovo: Recovering justice.* Lanham: Rowman & Littlefield.

Dreyfus, Paul. 2000. *Pol Pot, le bourreau du Cambodge.* Paris: Stock.

Drumbl, Mark A. 1999. Sobriety in a post-genocidal society: Good neighborliness among victims and aggressors in Rwanda? *Journal of Genocide Research* 1: 25-41.

Dudley, William. 2001. *Genocide.* San Diego: Greenhaven Press.

Dunne, Tim, and Daniela Kroslak. 2000. Genocide: Knowing what it is that we want to remember, or forget, or forgive. *International Journal of Human Rights* 4 (3-4): 27-46.

Dyregrov, Atle, Leila Gupta, Rolf Gjestad, and Eugenie Mukanoheli. 2000. Trauma exposure and psychological reactions to genocide among Rwandan children. *Journal of Traumatic Stress* 13 (1): 3-22.

Ellis, Stephen. 1999. *The mask of anarchy: The destruction of Liberia and the religious dimension of an African civil war.* New York: New York University Press.

Elovitz, Paul H. 1999. War, trauma, genocide, and Kosovo in the news and the classroom. *The Journal of Psychohistory* 27 (2): 188.

Fein, Helen. 1999. Genocide and gender: The uses of women and group destiny. *Journal of Genocide Research* 1:43-63.

Fleitz, Frederick H., Jr. 2002. *Peacekeeping fiascoes of the 1990s: Causes, solutions, and U.S. interests.* Westport, CT: Praeger Publishers.

Forman, Shep, and Patrick Stewart. 2000. *Good intentions: Pledges of aid for post-conflict recovery.* Boulder, CO: Lynne Rienner Publishers.

Fredholm, Michael. 2000. The prospects for genocide in Chechnya and extremist retaliation against the West. *Central Asian Survey* 19 (3-4): 315-328.

Freeman, Charles. 1998. *Crisis in Central Africa.* Chatham, NJ: Raintree Steck-Vaughn.

Friedrichs, David O. 1998. *State crime.* Brookfield, VT: Ashgate.

Friend, Melanie. 2001. *No place like home: Echoes from Kosovo.* San Francisco: Midnight Edition.

Frohardt, Mark, Diane Paul, and Larry Minear. 1999. *Protecting human rights: Challenge to humanitarian organizations.* Providence, RI: Thomas J. Watson Institute for International Studies, Brown University.

Gaudreault-DesBiens, Jean-François. 2000. From Sisyphus's dilemma to Sisyphus's duty? A meditation on the regulation of hate propaganda in relation to hate crimes and genocide. *McGill Law Journal* 46 (1): 121-140.

Giannakos, Symeon A., ed. 2002. *Ethnic conflict: Religion, identity, and politics.* Athens, OH: Ohio University Press.

Glenny, Misha. 2000. *The Balkans: Nationalism, war, and the Great Powers, 1804-1999.* New York: Viking.

Goldstone, Richard J. 1998. The role of the media in exposing crimes against humanity. *Media Studies Journal* 12:108.

———. 2000. *For humanity: Reflections of a war crimes investigator.* New Haven: Yale University Press.

Gordy, Eric D. 1999. *Culture of power in Serbia: Nationalism and the destruction of alternatives.* University Park, PA: Pennsylvania State University Press.

Gottesman, Evan R. 2002. *Cambodia after the Khmer Rouge: Inside the politics of nation building.* New Haven: Yale University Press.

Gourevitch, Philip. 1998. *We wish to inform you that tomorrow we will be killed with our families: Stories from Rwanda.* New York: Farrar, Straus and Giroux.

———. 1998. Annals of survival: The unimagined. *The New Yorker* 74:41.

———. 2000. Among the dead. In *Disturbing remains: Memory, history, and crisis in the twentieth century,* edited by M. S. Roth and C. G. Salas. Los Angeles: Getty Research Institute.

Greenawalt, Alexander K.A. 1999. Rethinking genocidal intent: The case for a knowledge-based interpretation. *Columbia Law Review* 99 (8): 2259.

Gutman, Roy, and David Rieff, eds. 1999. *Crimes of war: What the public should know.* New York: W.W. Norton & Company.

Hall, Harold V., and Leighton C. Whitaker, eds. 1999. *Collective violence: Effective strategies for assessing and interviewing in fatal group and institutional aggression.* Boca Raton, FL: CRC Press.

Hammarberg, Thomas. 2001. Efforts to establish a tribunal against KR leaders: Discussions between the Cambodian government and the UN. *The Phnom Penh Post,* September 14-27, 2001.

Harvey, John H. 2002. *Perspectives on loss and trauma: Assaults on the self.* Thousand Oaks, CA: Sage Publications.

Hayner, Priscilla B. 2002. *Unspeakable truths: Facing the challenge of truth commissions.* New York: Routledge.

Heder, Stephen R., and Brian D. Tittemore. 2001. *Seven candidates for prosecution: Accountability for the crimes of the Khmer Rouge.* Washington, DC: War Crimes Research Office, American University.

Heidenrich, John G. 2001. *How to prevent genocide: A guide for policymakers, scholars, and the concerned citizen.* Westport, CT: Praeger Publishers.

Helton, Arthur C. 2002. *The price of indifference: Refugees and humanitarian action in the new century.* Oxford: Oxford University Press.

Hiltermann, Joost R. 1991. The men who helped the man who gassed his own people. In *The Gulf war reader: History, documents, opinions,* edited by M. L. Sifry and C. Cerf. New York: Times Books.

Hintjens, Helen M. 1999. Explaining the 1994 genocide in Rwanda. *The Journal of Modern African Studies* 37 (2): 241.

Hinton, Alexander Laban. 1998. A head for an eye: Revenge in the Cambodian genocide. *American Ethnologist* 25:352.

———. 2002. *Annihilating difference: The anthropology of genocide.* Berkeley: University of California Press.

———. 2002. *Genocide: An anthropological reader.* Oxford: Blackwell.

Hirsch, Herbert. 2002. *Anti-genocide: Building an American movement to prevent genocide.* Westport, CT: Praeger Publishers.

Hitchens, Christopher. 2001. *The trial of Henry Kissinger.* New York and London: Verso.

Hoffman, Michael H. 2000. Emerging combatants, war crimes and the future of international humanitarian law. *Crime Law and Social Change* 34 (1): 99-110.

Hogg, Peter. 2001. *Crimes of war.* New York: Thomas Dunne Books.

Horowitz, Irving Louis. 2002. *Taking lives: Genocide and state power.* 4th ed. Rev. New Brunswick, NJ: Transaction Publishers.

Hukanovic, Rezak. 1996. *The tenth circle of hell: A memoir of life in the death camps of Bosnia.* 1st ed. New York: BasicBooks.

Human Rights Watch. 2001. *Under orders: War crimes in Kosovo.* New York: Human Rights Watch.

_____. 2001. Human Rights Watch World Report, 2001.

Human Rights Watch/Middle East. 1995. *Iraq's crime of genocide: the Anfal campaign against the Kurds, Human Rights Watch books.* New Haven: Yale University Press.

Hyde, Charles K. 2000. Casualty aversion: Implications for policy makers and senior military officers. *Airpower Journal* 14 (2):17-28.

Hyndman, Jennifer. 2000. *Managing displacement: Refugees and the politics of humanitarianism.* Minneapolis: University of Minneapolis Press.

Ignatieff, Michael. 1999. Balkan physics. *The New Yorker* 69.

_____. 2000. *Virtual war: Kosovo and beyond.* Toronto: Viking.

_____. 2001. *Human rights as politics and idolatry.* Princeton: Princeton University Press.

Immell, Myra. 2000. *Ethnic violence.* San Diego: Greenhaven Press.

International Commission on Intervention and State Sovereignty. 2001. *The responsibility to protect: Report of the International Commission on Intervention and State Sovereignty.* Ottawa: International Development Research Centre.

International Crisis Group. 2000. *Reality Demands: Documenting Violations of International Humanitarian Law in Kosovo.* Brussels: International Crisis Group.

_____. 2001. *International Criminal Tribunal for Rwanda: Justice delayed.* Nairobi, Arusha, and Brussels: International Crisis Group.

———. 2001. *The wages of sin: Confronting Bosnia's Republika Srpska*. Sarajevo and Brussels: International Crisis Group.

Jacobs, Alan. 1999. Power and survival: A preliminary explanation of genocide. *The Journal of Psychohistory* 27 (2): 180.

James, Patrick, and David Carment. 1998. *Peace in the midst of wars: Preventing and managing international ethnic conflicts*. Columbia, SC: University of South Carolina Press.

Janz, Mark, and Joann Slead, eds. 2000. *Complex humanitarian emergencies: Lessons from practitioners*. Monrovia, CA: World Vision.

Jeftemovas, Villia. 2001. *Brickyards turn to graveyards: From production to genocide in Rwanda*. Albany, NY: State University of New York Press.

Jennings, Christian. 2000. *Across the red river: Rwanda, Burundi and the heart of darkness*. London: Victor Gollancz.

Jentleson, Bruce W. 1999. *Opportunities missed, opportunities seized: Preventive diplomacy in the post-Cold War world*. Washington, DC: Carnegie Commission on Preventing Deadly Conflict.

Jett, Dennis. 2000. *Why peacekeeping fails*. New York: Palgrave.

Jokic, Aleksandar, ed. 2001. *War crimes and collective wrongdoing: A reader*. Malden, MA: Blackwell Publishers.

Jones, Adam. 2000. Gendercide and genocide. *Journal of Genocide Research* 2 (2): 185-211.

———. 2000. Kosovo: Orders of magnitude. *Idea: A Journal of Social Issues* 5 (1).

Jones, Bruce D. 2001. *Peacemaking in Rwanda: The dynamics of failure*. Boulder, CO: Lynne Rienner Publishers.

Judah, Tim. 2000. *Kosovo: War and revenge*. New Haven, CT: Yale University Press.

Kadric, Jusuf. 1999. *Brcko: Genocide and testimony*. Sarajevo: Institute for the research of crimes against humanity and international law.

Kallis, Aristotle A. 1999. Eliminationist crimes, state sovereignty and international intervention: The case of Kosovo. *Journal of Genocide Research* 1 (3): 417-438.

Kaplan, Jonathan. 2001. *The dressing station: A surgeon's chronicle of war and medicine*. New York: Grove Press.

Kaufman, Stuart J. 2001. *Modern hatreds: The symbolic politics of ethnic war.* Ithaca, NY: Cornell University Press.

Kaye, James, and Bo Strath. 2000. *Enlightenment and genocide, contradictions of modernity.* Bruxelles: P.I.E. Peter Lang.

Kecmanovic, Dusan. 2001. *Ethnic times: Exploring ethnonationalism in the Former Yugoslavia.* Westport, CT: Praeger Publishers.

Kellow, Christine, and Leslie Steeves. 1998. The role of radio in the Rwandan genocide. *Journal of Communication* 48:107.

Khan, Shaharyar M. 2000. *The shallow graves of Rwanda.* London: I.B. Tauris Publishers.

Kiernan, Ben. 1998. *The Pol Pot regime: Race, power, and genocide in Cambodia under the Khmer Rouge, 1975-79.* New Haven, CT: Yale University Press.

Kimenyi, Alexandre, and Otis L. Scott, eds. 2001. *Anatomy of genocide: State-sponsored mass-killings in the twentieth century.* Lewiston, NY: Edwin Mellen Press.

Klinghoffer, Arthur Jay. 1998. *The international dimension of genocide in Rwanda.* New York: New York University Press.

Kolodziej, Edward A. 2000. The Great Powers and genocide: Lessons from Rwanda. *Pacifica Review* 12 (2): 121-145.

Krog, Antjie. 1999. *Country of my skull: guilt, sorrow, and the limits of forgiveness in the new South Africa.* 1st U.S. ed. New York: Times Books.

Kuperman, Alan J. 2001. *The limits of humanitarian intervention: Genocide in Rwanda.* Washington, DC: Brookings Institution Press.

Kushner, Tony. 1999. *Refugees in an age of genocide: global, national, and local perspectives during the twentieth century.* England and Portland, OR: Frank Cass.

Lambeth, Benjamin S. 2001. *NATO's airwar for Kosovo.* Santa Monica: Rand.

Lawyers Committee for Human Rights. 1986. *Liberia, a promise betrayed: A report on human rights.* New York: Lawyers Committee for Human Rights.

Leatherman, Janie, William DeMars, Patrick D. Gaffney, and Raimo Väyrynen. 1999. *Breaking cycles of violence: Conflict prevention in intrastate crises.* West Hartford, CT: Kumarian Press.

Leurdijk, Dick, and Dick Zandee. 2001. *Kosovo: From crisis to crisis.* Aldershot, UK: Ashgate.

Levene, Mark. 2000. Why is the twentieth century the century of genocide? *Journal of World History* 11 (2): 305-336.

Linden, Sonja. 1999. Working with survivors of the Rwandan Genocide. *The Jewish Quarterly* 46 (2): 5.

Lorey, David E., and William H. Beezley, eds. 2002. *Genocide, collective violence, and popular memory: The politics of remembrance in the twentieth century.* Wilmington, DE: Scholarly Resources.

Loyd, Anthony. 2001. *My war gone by, I miss it so.* New York: Penguin Books.

Magas, Branka, and Ivo Zanic, eds. 2001. *The war in Croatia and Bosnia-Herzegovina, 1991-1995.* London and Portland, OR: Frank Cass.

Magnarella, Paul J. 2000. *Justice in Africa: Rwanda's genocide, its courts, and the UN Criminal Tribunal.* Aldershot, UK: Ashgate.

Makino, Uwe. 2001. Final solutions, crimes against mankind: On the genesis and criticism of the concept of genocide. *Journal of Genocide Research* 3 (1): 49-74.

Malcolm, Noel. 1998. *Kosovo: A short history.* New York: New York University Press.

Mam, Kalyanee E. 1999. *An oral history of family life under the Khmer Rouge.* New Haven, CT: Yale Center for International and Area Studies.

Mamdani, Mahmood. 2000. A brief history of genocide. *Transition* 87:26-47.

———. 2001. *When victims become killers: Colonialism, nativism and the genocide in Rwanda.* Oxford: James Currey.

McAllester, Matthew. 2002. *Beyond the mountains of the damned: The war inside Kosovo.* New York: New York University Press.

McCarthy, Patrick. 2000. *After the fall: Srebrenica survivors in St. Louis.* St. Louis, MO: Missouri Historical Society Press.

McCuen, Marnie J., ed. 2000. *The Genocide reader: The politics of ethnicity and extermination.* Hudson, WI: GEM Publications.

McIllwain, Jeffrey Scott. 2000. Introduction: Special issue: Criminology and genocide. *Crime, Law and Social Change* 34 (1): 1-6.

McNulty, Michael. 2000. French arms, war and genocide in Rwanda. *Crime, Law and Social Change* 33 (1-2): 105-129.

Meister, Robert. 1999. Forgiving and forgetting: Lincoln and the politics of national recovery. In *Human rights in political transitions: Gettysburg to Bosnia*, edited by C. A. Hesse and R. Post. New York: Zone Books.

Melvern, Linda. 2000. *A people betrayed: The role of the West in Rwanda's genocide.* London and New York: Zed Books.

Meredith, Martin. 1999. *Coming to terms: South Africa's search for truth.* 1st ed. New York: PublicAffairs.

Mertus, Julie. 1999. *Kosovo: How myths and truths started a war.* Berkeley: University of California Press.

Miller, Seumas. 1998. Collective responsibility, armed intervention and the Rwandan genocide. *International Journal of Applied Philosophy* 12:223.

Mills, Nicolaus, and Kira Brunner, eds. 2002. *The new killing fields: Massacre and the politics of intervention.* New York: BasicBooks.

Minow, Martha. 1998. *Between vengeance and forgiveness: Facing history after genocide and mass violence.* Boston: Beacon Press.

Mirkovic, Damir. 2000. The historical link between the Ustasha genocide and the Croato-Serb civil war: 1991-1995. *Journal of Genocide Research* 2 (3): 363-373.

National Security Archive Briefing Book. 2001. *The US and the genocide in Rwanda, 1994 evidence of inaction.* Washington, DC: National Security Archive.

Neier, Aryeh. 1998. *War crimes: Brutality, genocide, terror, and the struggle for justice.* New York: Times Books/Random House.

Neuffer, Elizabeth. 2001. *The key to my neighbor's house: Seeking justice in Bosnia and Rwanda.* 1st ed. New York: Picador.

Newbury, David. 1998. Understanding genocide. *African Studies Review* 41:73.

Norfolk, Simon, Harvey Benge, and Michael Ignatieff. 1999. *Genocide, memory, landscape.* Stockport, England: Dewi Lewis.

Organization of African Unity. 2000. International Panel of Eminent Personalities to Investigate the 1994 Genocide in Rwanda and the Surrounding Events.

Pajic, Zoran. 1998. A critical appraisal of human rights provisions of the Dayton Constitution of Bosnia and Herzegovina. *Human Rights Quarterly* 20:125-138.

Paust, Jordan. 1998. Individual criminal responsibility for human rights atrocities and sanction strategies. *Texas International Law Journal* 33 (3): 631-41.

Peck, Connie. 1998. *Sustainable peace: The role of the UN and regional organizations in preventing conflict*. Washington, DC: Carnegie Commission on Preventing Deadly Conflict.

Peterson, Scott. 2000. *Me against my brother: At war in Somalia, Sudan, and Rwanda: A journalist reports from the battlefields of Africa*. New York: Routledge.

Politi, Mauro, and Giuseppe Nesi, eds. 2001. *The Rome Statute of the International Criminal Court: A challenge to impunity*. Aldershot, UK: Ashgate.

Power, Samantha. 2002. *A problem from hell: America and the age of genocide*. New York: Basic Books.

Power, Samantha, and Graham T. Allison. 2000. *Realizing human rights: Moving from inspiration to impact*. New York: St. Martin's Press.

Prunier, Gérard. 1995. *The Rwanda crisis: History of a genocide*. New York: Columbia University Press.

——. 1999. *Rwanda in Zaire: From genocide to continental war*. London: C. Hurst & Co.

Quigley, John, Kenneth J. Robinson, and Howard J. De Nike, eds. 2000. *Genocide in Cambodia: Documents from the trial of Pol Pot and Leng Sary*. Philadelphia: University of Pennsylvania Press.

Randal, Jonathan C. 1997. *After such knowledge, what forgiveness? : My encounters with Kurdistan*. 1st ed. New York: Farrar, Straus and Giroux.

Reno, William. 1998. *Warlord politics and African states*. Boulder: Lynne Rienner Publishers.

Riemer, Neal, ed. 2000. *Protection against genocide: Mission impossible?* Westport, CT: Praeger Publishers.

Robben, Antonius C.G.M., and Marcelo M. Suarez-Orozco, eds. 2000. *Cultures under siege: Collective violence and trauma in interdisciplinary perspectives*. Cambridge: Cambridge University Press.

Rosand, Eric. 1998. The right to return under international law following mass dislocation: The Bosnia precedent? *Michigan Journal of International Law* 19 (4): 1091-1139.

Rubinstein, William D. 2001. Genocide surveyed. *International Journal of Human Rights* 5 (1): 113-129.

Russo, Charles J. 1998. At the table in Sarajevo: Reflections on ethnic segregation in Bosnia. *The Catholic Lawyer* 38:211.

Sacco, Joe. 2001. *Safe Area Gorazde: The war in eastern Bosnia, 1992-1995.* 3rd ed. Seattle, WA: Fantagraphics Book.

Salem, Richard A. 2000. *Witness to genocide, the children of Rwanda: Drawings by child survivors of the Rwandan genocide of 1994.* New York: Friendship Press.

Schabas, William. 2000. *Genocide in international law: The crime of crimes.* New York: Cambridge University Press.

_____, ed. 2001. *Introduction to the International Criminal Court.* Cambridge, UK and New York: Cambridge University Press.

_____. 2000. Groups protected by the Genocide Convention: Conflicting interpretations from the International Criminal Tribunal for Rwanda. *Ilsa Journal of International and Comparative Law* 6 (2): 375-388.

_____. 2000. Hate speech in Rwanda: The road to genocide. *McGill Law Journal* 46 (1): 141-172.

_____. 2001. Problems of international codification—Were the atrocities in Cambodia and Kosovo genocide? *New England Law Review* 35 (2): 287-302.

Scharf, Michael P. 1999. Justice in practice—Responding to Rwanda: Accountability mechanisms in the aftermath of genocide. *Journal of International Affairs* 52 (2): 621.

Scherrer, Christian P. 1999. Towards a theory of modern genocide. Comparative genocide research: Definitions, criteria, typologies, cases, key elements, patterns and voids. *Journal of Genocide Research* 1:13-23.

_____. 2001. *Genocide and crisis in Central Africa: Conflict roots, mass violence, and regional war.* Westport, CT: Praeger Publishers.

_____. 2002. *Structural prevention of ethnic violence.* New York: Palgrave.

Schulz, William. 2001. *In our own best interest: How defending human rights benefits us all.* Boston: Beacon Press.

Sewall, Sarah B., and Carl Kaysen. 2000. *The United States and the international criminal court: National security and international law.* Lanham, MD: Rowman & Littlefield.

Sharlach, Lisa. 1999. Gender and genocide in Rwanda: Women as agents and objects of genocide. *Journal of Genocide Research* 1 (3): 387-400.

Shattuck, John. 1999. Preventing genocide: Justice and conflict resolution in the post-Cold War world. *The Hofstra Law & Policy Symposium* 3:15.

Shaw, Jon A. 1998. Narcissism, identity formation and genocide. *Adolescent Psychiatry* 22:211.

Shawcross, William. 2000. *Deliver us from evil: Peacekeepers, warlords and a world of endless conflict.* London: Bloomsbury.

Silber, Laura, and Allan Little. 1997. *Yugoslavia: Death of a nation.* New York: Penguin Books.

Silove, Derrick. 1999. The psychological effects of torture, mass human rights violations, and refugee trauma: Toward an integrated conceptual framework. *Journal of Nervous and Mental Disease* 187 (4): 200.

Simon, Julius. 2000. Philosophy, genocide, and nationalism. *Contributions to the Study of Religion* 62:95-108.

Smith, David Norman. 1998. The psychocultural roots of genocide: Legitimacy and crisis in Rwanda. *The American Psychologist* 53-743.

Sokolovic, Dzemal, and Florian Bieber, eds. 2001. *Reconstructing multiethnic societies: The case of Bosnia-Herzegovina.* Aldershot, UK: Ashgate.

Spangenburg, Ray, and Diane Moser. 2000. *The crime of genocide: Terror against humanity.* Berkeley Heights, NJ: Enslow Publishers.

Staub, Ervin. 2000. Genocide and mass killing: Origins, prevention, healing and reconciliation. *Political Psychology* 21 (2): 367-382.

Steven, Lee A. 1999. Genocide and the duty to extradite or prosecute: Why the United States is in breach of its international obligations. *Virginia Journal of International Law* 39:425.

Stremlau, John. 1998. *People in peril: Human rights, humanitarian action, and preventing deadly conflict.* Washington, DC: Carnegie Commission on Preventing Deadly Conflict.

Sudetic, Chuck. 1998. *Blood and vengeance: One family's story of the war in Bosnia.* New York: W.W. Norton & Company.

Summers, Craig, and Eric Markusen. 1998. *Collective violence: Harmful behavior in groups and governments.* Lanham, MD: Rowman & Littlefield.

Thompson, Janna. 2002. *Taking responsibility for the past: Reparation and historical injustice.* Cambridge, UK and Malden, MA: Blackwell Publishers, Polity Press.

Tiefenbrun, Jonathan. 1999. Doctors and war crimes: Understanding genocide. *The Hofstra Law & Policy Symposium* 3:125.

Toggia, Pietro, Pat Lauderdale, and Abebe Zegeye. 2000. *Crisis and terror in the Horn of Africa: Autopsy of democracy, human rights and freedom.* Aldershot, UK: Ashgate.

Toope, Stephen J. 2000. Does international law impose a duty upon the United Nations to prevent genocide? *McGill Law Journal* 46 (1): 187-194.

Totten, Samuel. 1999. Human rights series—The scourge of genocide: Issues facing humanity today and tomorrow. *Social Education* 63:116.

Totten, Samuel, and Steven L. Jacobs. 2002. *Pioneers of genocide studies.* New Brunswick, NJ: Transaction Publishers.

United Nations High Commissioner for Refugees. 2000. *State of the world's refugees, 2000.* Oxford: Oxford University Press.

Uvin, Peter. 1998. *Aiding violence: The development enterprise in Rwanda.* West Hartford, CT: Kumarian Press.

_____. 2001. Difficult choices in the new post-conflict agenda: The international community in Rwanda after the genocide. *Third World Quarterly* 22:177-190.

Verdirame, Guglielmo. 2000. The genocide definition in the jurisprudence of the Ad Hoc Tribunals. *The International and Comparative Law Quarterly* 49 (3): 578.

Verwimp, Philip. 2000. Development ideology, the peasantry and genocide: Rwanda represented in Habyarimana's speeches. *Journal of Genocide Research* 2 (3): 325-361.

Vetlesen, Arne Johan. 1998. Impartiality and evil: A reconsideration provoked by genocide in Bosnia. *Philosophy & Social Criticism* 24:1.

_____. 2000. Genocide: A case for the responsibility of the bystander. *Journal of Peace Research* 37 (4): 519.

Vickers, Miranda. 1998. *Between Serb and Albanian: A history of Kosovo.* New York: Columbia University Press.

Wagner, Michele D. 1998. All the bourgmestre's men: making sense of genocide in Rwanda. *Africa Today* 45:25.

Waller, James. 2002. *Becoming evil: How ordinary people commit genocide and mass killing*. New York: Oxford University Press.

Wallimann, Isidor, and Michael N. Dobkowski. 2000 [1987]. *Genocide and the modern age: Etiology and case studies of mass death*. New York: Syracuse University Press.

Walter, Barbara F. 2002. *Committing to peace: The successful settlement of civil wars*. Princeton: Princeton University Press.

Weine, Stevan M. 1999. *When history is a nightmare: Lives and memories of ethnic cleansing in Bosnia-Herzegovina*. Piscataway, NJ: Rutgers University Press.

Westermeyer, Joseph. 2000. Health of Albanians and Serbians following the war in Kosovo: Studying the survivors of both sides of armed conflict. *JAMA: The Journal of the American Medical Association* 284 (5): 615.

Wheeler, Nicolas. 2001. *Saving strangers: Humanitarian intervention in international society*. New York: Oxford University Press.

Willis, Brian M., and Barry S. Levy. 2000. Recognizing the public health impact of genocide. *JAMA: The Journal of the American Medical Association* 284 (5): 612.

Windrich, Elaine. 1999. Revisiting genocide in Rwanda. *Third World Quarterly* 20 (4): 855.

Wippman, David, ed. 1998. *International law and ethnic conflict*. Ithaca, NY: Cornell University Press.

——. 1999. Atrocities, deterrence, and the elements of international justice. *Fordham International Law Journal* 23 (2): 473.

Wood, William B. 2001. Geographic aspects of genocide: A comparison of Bosnia and Rwanda. *Transactions* 26:57-77.

Yacoubian, George S. 2000. The (in)significance of genocidal behavior to the discipline of criminology. *Crime Law and Social Change* 34 (1): 7-19.

Yacoubian Jr., George S. 1999. The efficacy of international criminal justice: Evaluating the aftermath of the Rwandan genocide. *World Affairs* 161:186.